Continuity and Change on the United States Courts of Appeals

Continuity and Change on the United States Courts of Appeals

Donald R. Songer, Reginald S. Sheehan, and Susan B. Haire

Ann Arbor

THE UNIVERSITY OF MICHIGAN PRESS

Copyright © by the University of Michigan 2000
All rights reserved
Published in the United States of America by
The University of Michigan Press
Manufactured in the United States of America
⊚ Printed on acid-free paper

2003   2002   2001   2000   4   3   2   1

A CIP catalog record for this book is available from the British Library.

Library of Congress Cataloging-in-Publication Data

Songer, Donald R.
    Continuity and change on the United States Courts of Appeals /
Donald R. Songer, Reginald S. Sheehan, and Susan B. Haire.
        p.   cm.
    Includes bibliographical references and index.
    ISBN 0-472-11158-2 (cloth : alk. paper)
        1. Appellate courts—United States—History.   2. Judges—United States—
History.   3. Justice, Administration of—United States—History.
4. Judicial statistics—United States.   I. Sheehan, Reginald S., 1959–
II. Haire, Susan B.   III. Title.

KF8750 .S66   2000
347.73'24—dc21   00-037735

For Valorie, Michael, and Julie
DONALD R. SONGER

For Tracie, Kelsey, and Brennan
REGINALD S. SHEEHAN

For Rob, Alison, and Sara
SUSAN B. HAIRE

Contents

Figures

Tables

Preface

The United States Courts of Appeals have existed for more than a century as pivotal players in the creation and application of legal policy, the "vital center of the federal judicial system" (Howard 1981, 8). In spite of their importance, the courts of appeals exist at the very edge of the average American's consciousness if at all. They have been described by one leading text as the "least noticed of the regular constitutional courts" (Carp and Stidham 1991, 13). Nevertheless, over time, the policy-making role of the U.S. Courts of Appeals has shifted as the discretionary jurisdiction of the Supreme Court has changed and as new issues have come to the fore in the legal system. Thus, understanding the policy-making role of the U.S. Courts of Appeals requires an approach that appreciates the changing context of the judicial environment over time and by circuit. Our belief that no existing works adequately examined this shifting role of the courts of appeals led us first to seek a grant from the National Science Foundation to investigate the nature and extent of changes in these courts. Here, we present the first comprehensive analysis of the data set compiled to assess the evolving role of the U.S. Courts of Appeals over the twentieth century.

The Appeals Court Data Base

Following the initial proposal for the creation of an appeals court data base, the National Science Foundation funded a planning grant that brought together distinguished scholars from the law and courts community to design a data base that would serve the diverse needs of the law and social science community. After a year of development by the advisory board, a revised proposal was submitted to the National Science Foundation by Donald Songer to fund the creation of a multiuser data base of appeals court decisions. This proposal was funded with a grant from the NSF in 1989, and a new Board of Overseers was created. The data base of 15,315 cases was drawn from a random sample of published decisions by each circuit for each year during the period 1925 through 1988.

The Appeals Court Data Base Project was designed to create an extensive data set to facilitate the empirical analysis of the votes of judges and the decisions of the U.S. Courts of Appeals. In order to increase its utility for a wide variety of potential users, data on a broad range of variables of theoretical significance to public law scholars were coded. A major concern of the Board of Overseers was to ensure the collection of data over a sufficiently long period of time to encourage significant longitudinal studies of trends over time in the courts. Thus, the data base was designed to include cases decided as early as 1925 and ending in 1988. The year 1925 marks the beginning of an increased policy role for the courts of appeals brought about by the increase in the discretionary power of the Supreme Court over its docket, and it also marks the beginning of the second series of the *Federal Reporter*. The end date (1988) for the data base was dictated by the availability of data at the time the original proposal was submitted. Subsequently, the National Science Foundation funded a proposal for an update of the Appeals Court Data Base. The Appeals Court Data Base Project is available to interested scholars at the web page of the Program for Law and Judicial Politics at Michigan State University (http://www.ssc.msu.edu /~pls/pljp).

The data base includes a detailed coding of the nature of the issues presented; the statutory, constitutional, and procedural bases of the decision; the votes of the judges; and the nature of the litigants. The coding conventions employed in the collection of the data were designed to make comparisons to existing data sets on the Supreme Court and federal district courts with additional variables that are unique to this data set. These variables are grouped into four sections: basic case characteristics, participants, issues, and judges' votes.

Basic Case Characteristics

The first component, generally referred to as the *basic coding,* includes a series of miscellaneous variables that provide basic descriptive information about each case and its legal history. Included in this series of variables are the decision date, case citation, first docket number, the number of docket numbers resolved in the opinion, length of the opinion, the procedural history of the case, the circuit, the district and state of origin, a code for the district court judge who heard the case below, the type of district court decision appealed, the citation of the decision below, the identity of any federal regulatory agency that made a prior decision, the decision of the appeals court (e.g., affirmed, reversed, vacated), the number of dissents and concurrences, the number of amicus briefs filed, the nature of the counsel on each side, whether the case was reviewed by the Supreme Court, and whether the case involved a class action, cross appeals, or an *en banc* decision.

Participants

The appeals court data base provides very detailed information about the parties involved in each case. Litigants are categorized into seven basic types (natural persons, private business, nonprofit groups or associations, federal government and its agencies, state governments and their agencies, units of local government, and fiduciaries or trustees). Each of the seven general categories is then broken down further into a number of specific categories. These codes for the detailed nature of the litigants were recorded for the first two appellants and the first two respondents. In addition, the data base records the number of appellants and respondents, matches the appellant and respondent to the plaintiff and defendant in the original action, notes whether any of the formally listed litigants were intervenors, and indicates if any of the original parties with actual substantive adverse interests are not listed among the formally named litigants.

It is impossible to list all of the detailed litigant categories in a short overview, but two examples may illustrate the nature of the detail available. The private business category is broken down into seventy-seven specific types of business (e.g., oil and gas mining or extraction, residential construction, chemical manufacturing). Then, each of these seventy-seven types is categorized as to whether or not it was bankrupt and what the scope of its operations were (i.e., clearly local, clearly national or international, intermediate scope, impossible to determine scope). Thus, there are 616 possible categories for private business litigants. The natural person codes record the gender of the litigant, a detailed ethnic categorization, citizenship (U.S. or other), and the income status (definite evidence that litigant is poor, presumed poor, above the poverty line but not clearly wealthy, presumed wealthy—high status job, clear indication of wealth, not ascertained).

Issues

Three types of variables were coded in order to capture the nature of the issues in the case. First, the appeals court data base includes a traditional categorization of issues that parallels the issue categories in the Spaeth Supreme Court Data Base (these variables are denoted as CASETYP1 and

CASETYP2). These issues (case types) capture the nature of the dispute that led to the original suit. Eight general categories (criminal, civil rights, First Amendment, due process, privacy, labor relations, economic activity and regulation, and miscellaneous) are subdivided into a total of 220 specific issue categories. For example, specific categories include due process rights of prisoners, denial of fair hearing or notice in government employment disputes, union organizing, motor vehicle torts, insurance disputes, government regulation of securities, admiralty—personal injury, and immigration. For each of these case types, the directionality of the court's decision was recorded, using conventional definitions of directionality that are analogous to those in the Spaeth Supreme Court Data Base. For most, but not all issue categories, these will correspond to notions of liberalism and conservatism that are commonly used in the public law literature. For example, decisions supporting the position of the defendant in a criminal procedure case, the plaintiff who asserts a violation of her First Amendment rights, and the secretary of labor who sues a corporation for violation of child labor regulations are all coded as "liberal."

A second approach to capture the issues was utilized in a series of variables that were coded from the head notes describing the West Topics and key numbers at the beginning of each case. From these head notes, the two most frequently cited constitutional provisions, titles, and sections of the U.S. Code, federal rules of civil/criminal procedure were coded. This coding should be useful for scholars interested in the application and interpretation of specific elements of law.

Finally, the issues in each case were coded from the standpoint of the judge who wrote the opinion of the court. Each of the sixty-nine variables in this section was coded in terms of an issue question. For each variable, coders indicated whether or not the issue was discussed in the opinion. If the opinion discussed the issue, the resolution of the issue was also recorded (generally whether the issue was resolved in favor of the position of the appellant or the respondent). All issues discussed in the opinion were recorded (i.e., finding that a given issue was discussed did not preclude the conclusion that any other issue was discussed as well). The first set of these variables recorded whether a series of threshold issues was addressed (e.g., standing, failure to state a claim, mootness, jurisdiction). Each case also was coded for whether or not the opinion engaged in statutory construction, the interpretation of the Constitution, or the interpretation of court doctrine or circuit law. In addition to these variables that are common to most cases, a long series of variables was used to capture whether the court dealt with specific questions relating to the relevant area of law. For example, in criminal cases, several issue variables dealt with questions of criminal procedure (e.g., was there prejudicial conduct by the prosecutor, was there a challenge to jury instructions, was there a challenge to the admissibility of evidence from a search and seizure, did the court rule on the sufficiency of evidence). Some cases between private parties focused on questions relating to civil disputes (e.g., was the validity of an injunction at issue, was there an issue relating to discovery procedures), whereas other cases involved issues relating to the action of the government (e.g., was the application of the substantial evidence rule questioned, did the agency fail to develop an adequate record).

Judges and Votes

The final section of the data set includes the identity of judges participating on the appeals court panel and the directionality of their votes. A five-digit code was created to identify every appeals court judge (including judges on senior status) and every district court judge who participated on an appeals court panel during the period of the data base. Judges from other courts (e.g., retired Supreme Court justices, judges of the Federal Circuit, judges of the Court of Customs and Patents Appeals) who served on appeals court panels were not coded and are treated as missing data. The judge codes for the appeals court data are structured so that the decisional data on each judge can be merged with the personal attribute and background data on each judge collected by Professors Deborah Barrow, Gerard Gryski, and Gary Zuk at Auburn University.

The Appeals Court Data Base project represents a significant commitment of money by the Law and Social Sciences program of the NSF. From its conception it was designed to create a data base for the benefit of the entire constituency of the Law and Social Science program. The NSF anticipated that the data base created by this grant would be of tremendous benefit and interest to a very wide spectrum of our members. The Board of Overseers took special pains to ensure that the project was designed in such a way that it would serve the interests of the widest group of scholars possible. The data base is arguably one of the richest available to public law scholars.

Reliability Analysis

The detailed description of variables in the documentation of the data base reports the results of an analysis of intercoder reliability performed before the data base was released. To check the reliability of the coding, a random sample of 250 cases was selected from the 15,315 cases in the data base. This sample of 250 cases was then independently coded by a second coder and the results of the two codings were compared. Three measures of reliability are reported. First, the simple rate of agreement (expressed as a percentage) between the code assigned by the first coder and the code assigned by the second coder is reported. In addition, two bivariate measures of association are reported: gamma and Kendall's tau-c. Kendall's tau-c is most appropriate for variables that have an ordinal level of measurement. Therefore, users should exercise caution in interpreting the meaning of this statistic for variables that are not ordinal. Nevertheless, for some of the variables that can take many values (e.g., CASETYP1), even though the values of the variable are not completely ordinal, many of the values that are close to each other are more similar to each other than they are to values that are numerically distant from them. For such variables, high values of tau will indicate that many of the disagreements in coding were between values that were numerically close.

A few of the variables have rates of agreement that are very high (e.g., above 96 percent) but still have low or even negative values of gamma and/or tau. All of these variables have highly skewed distributions. The high rates of agreements indicate that for most cases both coders agreed that the variable was in its modal value (typically these were issue variables with a modal value of zero, which indicated that the issue was not discussed in the case) but in the small number of cases in which one of the coders felt that the variable did not fall into the modal category, the second coder generally disagreed.

The Present Study

This study examines changes in the courts of appeals over a sixty-four-year period from 1925 to 1988. The analysis is based on the recently released United States Courts of Appeals Data Base described above (a complete list of the variables in the data base is provided in the appendix). Particular attention is given to changes in the kinds of people who have served as judges on the courts of appeals, the evolution in the agenda of the cases they have decided, differences over time in the nature of the litigants who have used the courts of appeals, who wins and who loses in each decade, and patterns of decision making that have characterized the courts.

Acknowledgments

The writing of this book in many ways reflects the culmination of a decade of work in which we accumulated many debts to colleagues who provided their service at critical junctures. Perhaps most importantly, we acknowledge the dedication and high degree of professionalism provided by a virtual army of students who worked endless hours in the collection of the data for the Appeals Court Data Base. In particular, we express our heartfelt appreciation to Julia Allen, Yolanda Barreros, Kelly Boozer, Lisbeth Bosshart, Sherral Brown-Guinyard, Jay Cain, Trish Collins, Kelley Crews-Meyer, Kathleen Dougherty, Kevin Eberle, Venelin Ganev, Wendy Goodwin, Linda Hatcher, Norman Hayes, Amy Henry, Rob Herron, Jenny Anderson Horne, Martha Humphries, Tammie Jackson, Richard Jimenez, Kristine Johannesmeyer, Dan Johnson, Erin Kaheny, Stefanie Lindquist, Valerie Palmer, Kristina Pray, Kirk Randazzo, Ben Reed, Lisa Richey, Tammy Sarver, Denise Howard Stevens, Valerie Sulfaro, Tracy Tisdale-Clawson, Anne Wilson, and Lee Wilson. We are especially grateful to Ashlyn Kuersten who organized and supervised the day-to-day operations of the data collection for over three years.

We appreciate the generous support provided by the National Science Foundation that made possible the Appeals Court Data Base and, ultimately, this book. A special thanks is in order to Felice Levine, former director of the Law and Social Sciences Program of the National Science Foundation, who initially had the faith to fund the project, and to Neal Tate, who helped to shepherd the project to completion during his tenure with NSF. We received valuable suggestions and guidance from many of our colleagues during the development of the project, including an initial advisory board consisting of Burton Atkins (Florida State University), Paul Burstein (University of Washington), Gregory Caldeira (Ohio State), Bradley C. Canon (University of Kentucky), Robert A. Carp (University of Houston), Sheldon Goldman (University of Massachusetts), and Lettie Wenner (University of Illinois at Chicago). The project also benefited immensely from the long hours and helpful advice provided by the Board of Overseers created by the National Science Foundation, consisting of Gregory Caldeira (Ohio State University), Deborah Barrow (Auburn University), Micheal Giles (Emory University), Lawrence Friedman (Stanford Law School), Donna Stienstra (Federal Judicial Center), and Neal Tate (University of North Texas). While not formally a member of any advisory board, Harold J. Spaeth generously provided much helpful advice, especially on the problems of working with large data bases and with some of the details of coding court opinions.

CHAPTER 1

The Courts of Appeals in the American Judicial Structure

Introduction

In 1973, the Equal Employment Opportunity Commission (EEOC) initiated an investigation against Sears, Roebuck and Co., the largest civilian employer of women in the United States. Eleven years later, the EEOC sued Sears under Title VII of the Civil Rights Act of 1964, alleging the employer had engaged in sex discrimination in its hiring and promotion practices. Basing their suit on statistical evidence, the EEOC claimed that Sears did not hire and promote proportionate numbers of women in sales positions. In their defense, Sears claimed that women were generally not interested in commission sales work. The federal district court judge did not accept the statistical evidence offered by the EEOC as evidence of intentional discrimination and agreed with Sears, dismissing the charges. In *EEOC v. Sears*, 839 F.2d 302 (1988), the Seventh Circuit affirmed the decision of the district court. Writing for the majority, Judge Harlington Wood noted that "the reasons for women's lack of interest in commission selling included a fear or dislike of what they perceived as cut-throat competition, increased pressure and risk associated with commission sales. Noncommission selling, on the other hand, was associated with more social contact and friendship, less pressure and less risk" (839 F.2d 302, at 321). Not surprisingly, this decision sparked substantial debate in the legal community and, in some instances, criticism from judges in other circuits.[1] For example, in a similar case decided the following year, the Ninth Circuit opted to "reject the approach taken by the Sears majority which places a very heavy—and possibly insurmountable—burden on the plaintiff" (885 F.2d 575, at 581). In addition, the Seventh Circuit's opinion in the Sears case raised issues for legal scholars that ranged from questions regarding the use of statistical evidence in employment discrimination claims to concerns raised by feminist jurisprudents over gender-based stereotypes in the workplace.[2] The decision was not reviewed by the Supreme Court, and as this discussion suggests, several circuits adopted different approaches to the same issue. Clearly, the effect of the Sears case extended beyond the litigants and the boundaries of the circuit to policymakers, employers, and workers throughout the United States.

The important policy-making role of the U.S. Courts of Appeals is not a recent phenomenon. As early as the 1920s and 1930s, a lower federal court judge established a reputation as being a leader in the development of law in several areas, particularly those relating to the interpretation of federal statutes and disputes associated with commercial relations. This judge, Learned Hand, was never appointed to the U.S. Supreme Court, but his opinions as a judge on the Second Circuit were cited and quoted in courts throughout the country, including the U.S. Supreme Court.[3] For example, many judges have cited Judge Hand's opinions offering guidance on how to approach statutory interpretation. As noted by Justice Stevens of the Supreme Court in a recent concurring opinion, Judge Hand had advised that "statutes should be construed, not as theorems of Euclid, but with some imagination of the purposes which lie behind them."[4] Judge Hand's writings also were influential in the development of law dealing with patents, trademark rights, and intellectual property. He established the principle that inventors who have decided to lift the veil of secrecy from their work must choose either the protection of a federal patent or the dedication of their idea to the public at large. In an oft-cited passage authored by Judge Hand, "it is a condition upon the inventor's right to a patent that he shall not exploit his discovery competitively after it is ready for patenting; he must content himself with either secrecy or legal monopoly" (*Metallizing Engineering Co. v. Kenyon Bearing and Auto Parts Co.*, 153 F.2d 516 [2d Cir., 1946]). During these early years, opinions of lower federal court judges, including Judge Hand, influenced the commercial sector and in many ways set the parameters for business practices that continue today.

As these examples illustrate, understanding the policy-making role of the U.S. Courts of Appeals requires an approach that appreciates the changing context of the judicial environment over time and by circuit. Judge Hand's role in the development of commercial law was necessary, in part because the commercial sector was rapidly evolving in the northeastern states within the Second Circuit, giving rise to disputes for which there was no firm precedent. His focus on economic issues, particularly "staple" litigation, including contracts, patents, and trademark disputes, reflected the kinds of claims being litigated in the federal courts during the early part of this century. Over time, the policy-making role of the U.S. Courts of

Appeals has shifted. Civil rights cases raising issues such as those in the Sears case have become more commonplace in the lower federal courts. In a recent account describing work on an appellate court, Judge Coffin of the First Circuit described the rise of civil rights cases as illustrated through a series of computer searches (Coffin 1994). In a search of cases decided before 1950, Judge Coffin could not find any decisions that dealt with the Civil Rights Act of 1866 (42 U.S.C. Sec. 1983). He found that 159 had been decided by 1960, but by the end of 1991, the number of Sec. 1983 cases had climbed to 44,148. In addition to changes in the issues being litigated, jurists on the U.S. Courts of Appeals in the 1970s and 1980s have seen an explosion in the number of cases being appealed (see fig. 1.2).

The average American is barely aware (if at all) of the courts of appeals, in spite of their importance. They have been described by one leading text as the "least noticed of the regular constitutional courts" (Carp and Stidham 1991, 13). They receive little media coverage because their decisions are often less dramatic than the pronouncements of the Supreme Court. However, as the cases described above illustrate, one should not assume from this lack of attention that the courts of appeals are unimportant players in the American political system. In fact, the courts of appeals occupy a pivotal position, the "vital center of the federal judicial system," according to Howard (1981, 8). Their traditional role of ensuring uniformity in national law has been important since their creation in the 1890s; it has become vital in an era in which the number of cases being litigated in the federal courts has risen substantially, with the Supreme Court reviewing fewer than one of every two thousand decisions of the district courts (Songer 1991). Their role in providing judicial oversight of federal regulatory agencies grows in importance as federal regulation of the economy continues to become ever more pervasive. Cases with major economic impact are no longer framed exclusively as constitutional issues but increasingly as issues of regulatory detail that are not at the center of the Supreme Court's agenda. As the final authoritative policymakers in the interpretation of many areas of federal law, these courts are major political institutions that function not only as norm enforcers but also as important creators of public policy. Finally, the courts of appeals continue to play an essential role as federal judges balance the pressures emanating from the need for national policy coherence against the centrifugal forces and local perspectives inherent in a decentralized political system. Any adequate understanding of the American legal system thus requires systematic investigation of these "least noticed" courts and their judges.

The present study examines changes in the courts of appeals over a sixty-four-year period from 1925 to 1988. The analysis is based on the recently released United States Courts of Appeals Data Base. Particular attention is given to changes in the kinds of people who have served as judges on the courts of appeals, the evolution in the agenda of the cases they have decided, differences over time in the nature of the litigants who have used the courts of appeals, who wins and who loses in each decade, and patterns of decision making that have characterized the courts.

The Evolution of the Courts of Appeals

The provision in the U.S. Constitution for lower federal courts is "deceptively simple" (Richardson and Vines 1970, 18). In addition to the requirement that there be a single Supreme Court, the Constitution stipulates that there will be "such inferior courts as Congress may from time to time ordain and establish."[5] The deliberate vagueness of this constitutional formulation reflects the inability of the convention, divided between advocates of states' rights versus supporters of a strong national government, to agree on the precise organization and structure of the lower courts. Consequently, they compromised by leaving the details to be worked out by other politicians in future Congresses (Carp and Stidham 1998).

The vagueness of the constitutional language postponed the struggle over the structure of the federal courts only until the first Congress met. Many important questions were left unresolved by the Constitution, including whether the new federal courts would engulf state judiciaries and whether English common-law rights of individuals would be protected (Marcus and Wexler 1992). After a heated debate, the Judiciary Act of 1789 emerged, providing the first definition of federal court structure. In that initial system, a six-member Supreme Court was created along with three circuit courts and thirteen district courts. The district courts were trial courts presided over by a single district judge, sitting alone. Each circuit court was staffed by two Supreme Court justices and one district judge.[6] Although the first circuit courts had some appellate responsibilities, they were primarily trial courts. Appeals could go to the Supreme Court from either the three-judge panels of the circuit courts or from the single-judge district courts. Appeal to the Supreme Court from both sets of lower courts was a matter of right rather than at the discretion of the Supreme Court.

While this initial structure was never viewed as completely satisfactory,[7] several basic principles were established that have persisted to the present (Richardson and Vines 1970, 21). First, the jurisdictions of both the district courts and the circuit courts were drawn along state lines. No district boundaries crossed state lines.[8] Second, each federal district judge was a resident of his state and held court only in his home state. Third, the circuit court was organized with a regional rather than with a national focus. Finally, the district and circuit courts were organized as courts of general jurisdiction serving a geographic area rather than as specialized courts with jurisdiction over particular types of cases.

Throughout much of the nineteenth century, conflict between nationalists and states' rights advocates continued over the structure and jurisdiction of the lower federal courts. While the debate continued, the absence of any true intermediate appellate court contributed to an unmanageable volume of mandatory appeals on the Supreme Court docket. Various "stopgap" measures were attempted with little success until Congress passed the Evarts Act in 1891 (Posner 1985). This act, which marked the "final victory" of the pro-national power advocates, created the courts of appeals to relieve the Supreme Court's burden of hearing all appeals (Richardson and Vines 1970). The new courts would hear most appeals from existing trial courts and exercise the full range of federal jurisdiction granted by the Constitution. Additional legislation passed in 1911 and 1925 simplified the federal court structure by abolishing the old circuit courts (leaving the district courts as the sole trial court of general jurisdiction) and codifying the role of the Supreme Court as a tribunal that would have largely discretionary appellate jurisdiction.

The basic structure of the federal courts, which has undergone only minor alteration since the passage of the "Judges Bill" of 1925, has three levels. At the bottom, the district courts act as the basic trial courts for virtually the entire range of federal jurisdiction. Ninety-one geographically defined judicial districts, none of which has boundaries that cross state lines,[9] are typically presided over by a single judge.[10] The same judges hear both civil and criminal cases and often preside over trials with juries.

The second level of the federal judicial system is composed of the U.S. Courts of Appeals. Since the passage of the Evarts Act in 1891, the numbered circuit courts of appeals have been organized regionally, with three to nine states falling within each circuit. Each circuit court has jurisdiction over all the judicial districts within its geographical boundaries. No state is split between different circuits, and with the exception of states and territories outside the continental United States, circuit boundaries define geographically contiguous areas (see fig. 1.1 and table 1.1). In the original structure created in 1891, there were nine numbered regional circuits. In 1893, a separate circuit was created for the District of Columbia. Two circuits have undergone splits in the subsequent years: in 1929, the Tenth Circuit was carved out of the old Ninth Circuit, and in 1981, the Eleventh Circuit was formed by splitting the old Fifth Circuit. More recently, there has been active consideration of proposals to divide the Ninth Circuit, but as yet no action has been taken.

While changes in the boundaries of circuits may seem mundane, even simple splits in existing circuits to accommodate increasing caseloads often involves intense political conflict. For example, the division of the old Fifth Circuit in 1981 came only after nearly two decades of sometimes bitter controversy. During that period, the proposal to divide the circuit evoked heated debate among members of Congress, lobbyists from civil rights groups, and the judges themselves who were as concerned about a broad range of judicial *policies,* including the ramifications of the proposed split on efforts to desegregate public schools in the region, as they were about judicial efficiency and administrative coherence (Barrow and Walker 1988).

The Supreme Court has remained the highest appellate court from the beginning of the republic. Its size has fluctuated from the six justices authorized by the Judiciary Act of 1790 to ten for a brief period following the Civil War, before stabilizing at nine justices throughout the twentieth century. The nine justices sit *en banc* to decide all cases decided on the merits using a majority-vote decision rule. The Constitution provides for the High

TABLE 1.1.   **Circuit Boundaries of the United States Courts of Appeals**

Circuit	Geographical Boundaries
First	Maine, Massachusetts, New Hampshire, Puerto Rico, Rhode Island
Second	Connecticut, New York, Vermont
Third	Delaware, New Jersey, Pennsylvania, Virgin Islands
Fourth	Maryland, North Carolina, South Carolina, Virginia, West Virginia
Fifth	Louisiana, Mississippi, Texas
Sixth	Kentucky, Michigan, Ohio, Tennessee
Seventh	Illinois, Indiana, Wisconsin
Eighth	Arkansas, Iowa, Minnesota, Missouri, Nebraska, North Dakota, South Dakota
Ninth	Alaska, Arizona, California, Guam, Hawaii, Idaho, Montana, Nevada, Oregon, Washington, N. Mariana Islands
Tenth	Colorado, Kansas, New Mexico, Oklahoma, Utah, Wyoming
Eleventh	Alabama, Florida, Georgia
DC	District of Columbia

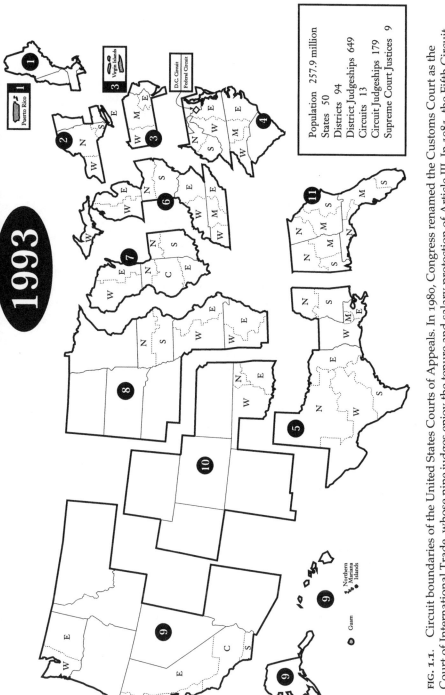

FIG. 1.1. Circuit boundaries of the United States Courts of Appeals. In 1980, Congress renamed the Customs Court as the Court of International Trade, whose nine judges enjoy the tenure and salary protection of Article III. In 1981, the Fifth Circuit was divided into the Fifth and Eleventh Circuits. In 1982, Congress created the Federal Circuit, with its own court of appeals, a jurisdictional rather than a geographic circuit, out of the Court of Claims and the Court of Customs and Patent Appeals. The Canal Zone district court closed on March 31, 1982.

Court to hear a few cases in its original jurisdiction,[11] but the bulk of its agenda is filled with requests to review the decisions of the circuit courts of appeals and federal law questions arising from decisions of the highest court in each state. Since 1925, the Court has had nearly complete control over its appellate docket and now rejects more than 97 percent of the requests for review.

The Modern U.S. Courts of Appeals

The U.S. Courts of Appeals exercise only appellate jurisdiction. They are responsible for reviewing all cases appealed from the decisions of the federal district courts within their boundaries as well as the appeals from the decisions of a wide spectrum of federal administrative agencies.[12] Although the Supreme Court has had a substantial degree of discretionary control over its docket since 1925, the courts of appeals have no such luxury. Instead, appeals court judges must address every case in which the losing litigant in the district court or administrative agency decides to appeal. Under long-standing principles of the common law, all losing litigants in civil cases and criminal defendants who lose at trial have a right to one appeal. At least when the costs of appeals are minimal,[13] some litigants may decide to take their case to the U.S. Courts of Appeals even if they have a negligible chance of winning on appeal. As a result of this absence of docket control, many of the appeals coming to the courts of appeals are "easy" cases that result in the routine affirmation of the decision below.[14]

The courts typically sit in panels of three judges with membership on the panels rotating among all of the judges appointed to a circuit.[15] On most panels, all three members are appeals court judges in active service in the circuit in question. However, in more than a quarter of the cases one of the judges assigned to serve on the panel will be a district court judge, an appeals court judge from another circuit, or an appeals court judge on "senior" status.[16] On occasion, the third judge is drawn from other federal courts (e.g., the Court of Customs and Patent Appeals, the Court of Appeals for the Federal Circuit, or retired justices from the Supreme Court). Formally, the chief judge of the circuit[17] assigns members to panels, though the practice is generally for the clerk to assign members to panels randomly. The panel rotation system generally ensures that all judges within a circuit will sit together on the same panel at some point in their tenure on the bench.

The first step in the appellate process is for the losing party in the district court (or administrative agency) to file a notice of an intent to appeal.

The trial court loser (now designated as the "appellant") then proceeds to do three things: assemble the record appendix for the appeal, specify a list of errors alleged to have been made during the trial, and write a brief to argue the specifications of error. According to Judge Coffin of the First Circuit, the assembling of the record is often viewed as a "very low-level, grubby piece of work" (1994, 104). It entails assembling, organizing, and presenting all of the factual material from the official record of the trial (portions of the transcript of testimony and so on) in a manner that will most efficiently provide the appeals court judges' access to the factual basis of the allegations argued in the appellant's brief. Although the process of preparing the record appears mundane, appeals are often won or lost on the basis of how effectively the facts of the case are presented. Once the record is compiled, the appellant will specify a series of errors that the trial judge is alleged to have made as the basis for overturning the lower court's decision. These specifications must then be supported with a brief that develops in detail a series of legal arguments to justify the allegations contained in the specification of errors. The court will typically only consider allegations of error that are supported by arguments in the brief. Copies of the record, specifications of error, and the brief are sent to each judge assigned to sit on the three-judge panel hearing the case and to opposing counsel. Opposing counsel (representing the trial court winner, now referred to as the *appellee* or *respondent*) is then permitted to file an opposing brief that details arguments for affirming the decision of the trial court or administrative agency. After appellant's counsel receives the respondent's brief, they may elect to write a second brief, known as a *reply brief*, in which they attempt to counter the legal arguments raised in the respondent's brief.

Once all the motions and briefs have been received, the real work of the court begins. Before any further proceedings involving the litigants are conducted, the judges will screen the cases on their docket to determine if any cases can be disposed of in an expeditious fashion. During this screening, the judges decide whether to give an appeal a full review with oral argument or to summarily dispose of the matter. In some circuits, this informal screening is conducted primarily by staff attorneys. Since the late 1960s, the increased utilization of these screening procedures has made appeals court judges' work load more manageable. Prior to 1970, approximately a quarter of all appeals were terminated without a formal hearing (usually by dismissal of the appeal or summary affirmance of the trial court's decision) after this initial screening. However, in the 1970s and 1980s this rate of procedural termination increased to 46 percent of all appeals (Carp and Stidham 1998). Once the court has decided on such a procedural termination, a brief order will be sent to the litigants, but the judges will not issue a published opinion to explain their decision.

For cases that survive the initial screening, a formal hearing will be held. But before this hearing, much of the detailed analysis of the litigants' arguments will take place. Central to the processing of litigant demands is the relationship between each judge and his or her law clerks.[18] Generally, a clerk assigned to each case will be expected to analyze each of the briefs in detail, check each reference in the briefs to materials in the trial record, and then research independently the central points of law in question. The product of this research will be a bench memorandum to their judge that analyzes the strengths and weaknesses of each litigant's position and highlights important points to pursue during oral argument.

The hearing itself will be open to the public. At the hearing, attorneys for both the appellant and the respondent will be invited to argue their position orally before the three-judge panel. The amount of time allocated for this oral argument is at the discretion of the judges. Most commonly, each side is given thirty minutes to present their case, but some arguments are limited to as little as ten minutes. Judges will prepare for the arguments by studying the briefs submitted by each side and often by reading memorandums prepared by the judges' law clerks[19] that summarize and analyze the arguments and the factual record in the case. During the argument, the attorneys may be frequently interrupted by questions from the judges.

Each time a panel of three judges is constituted by the chief judge of the circuit, they typically meet together for a week at some location within the circuit. During that week, the panel is likely to hear arguments in twenty to thirty cases that have been randomly assigned to the panel by the court clerk. After hearing oral arguments, the judges hold a private meeting, called a *conference*, to discuss the week's cases. After discussing each case, the judges tentatively vote either to affirm or reverse the decision below. All decisions are by majority vote. After deciding the outcome of the case, the judges must decide whether the issues in the case are important enough to warrant the publication of an opinion explaining the court's decision. While the precise rules governing when an opinion should be published vary by circuit, they generally specify that only decisions that will make a contribution to the body of law of the circuit—that is, only those decisions that create new precedent or modify existing precedent—should be accompanied by a published opinion. In recent years, the rate of publication has fallen so that only a third of all appeals court decisions are accompanied by published opinions. Other decisions will be announced in brief written orders that will be sent to the parties in the case and will be maintained as public records in the office of the court clerk. Published opinions are available in all law school libraries (and many other libraries) in a series of volumes published under the title *The Federal Reporter.*

For each decision that is to be accompanied by a published opinion, a member of the majority is assigned to prepare a draft of an opinion of the court that will announce the court's decision and explain the legal basis for the decision. The appeals court judge on the panel with the most seniority in the circuit (excluding judges on "senior status") makes the assignment of who will write the opinion of the court, unless the senior judge dissented from the majority position. In that case, the senior judge in the majority assigns the opinion. After the conference, the judges return to their home offices (which may be in different cities within the circuit) to work on writing the opinions they have been assigned. Most judges consider opinion writing to be the most important part of their work because the court's decision will make new law or clarify existing law for those in the legal community. Opinion writing is also the most time-consuming aspect of the judges' work. Strict confidentiality is maintained about the outcome of conference deliberations until the opinions are completed and released to the public. The first draft of the opinion is typically the product of intense interaction between the judge authoring the opinion and one or more of the judge's clerks. Once a draft of an opinion is completed, the author will circulate it to the other two judges who may suggest additions, deletions, or other modifications. Opinions often go through multiple drafts before they are released, and judges who voted for or against the prevailing party in conference may, and sometimes do, change sides during the opinion-drafting process. The vote in conference is considered to be only a tentative decision; the decision is not official until an opinion of the court, supported by a majority of the panel, is released. The opinion-writing process has no set time limits and sometimes takes several months to complete after oral arguments. Once issued, the opinion becomes the law of the circuit, which is legally binding on all district and appeals court judges within the circuit.

En Banc Review

While the U.S. Courts of Appeals normally convene as three-judge panels, on occasion all appeals court judges in the circuit will sit together to decide a decision *en banc.* Given the large number of active judges in some circuits,

Congress has provided that these courts will develop internal operating procedures that will provide for "limited" *en banc* review. In most circuits, a vote on *en banc* review occurs only after a party has been denied a rehearing by the panel, but one member of the panel has agreed with the litigant's suggestion for a rehearing *en banc* (McFeeley 1987). A decision to proceed *en banc* generally requires a favorable vote from a majority of the active judges in the circuit, and all decisions of the court sitting *en banc* are by majority vote. In addition to the Federal Rules of Appellate Procedure (FRAP), circuit internal operating procedures tend to discourage its use. The criteria for rehearing *en banc* are generally vague, suggesting rehearing is appropriate when necessary to secure intracircuit uniformity in its decisions or when the decision is an "exceptionally important" one (FRAP 35). Judicial scholars have long noted the limited use of *en banc* review (McFeeley 1987; Howard 1981). In fact, one recent survey of empirical studies concludes that courts have consistently resolved fewer than 1 percent of their cases *en banc* (George 1999, 214).

In the rare instances in which a circuit does sit to review a decision *en banc*, the results are often significant. Perhaps most important, *en banc* proceedings are sometimes used to overturn policy decisions of panels that are contrary to the preferences of the circuit majority. For example, a recent *en banc* decision of the Fourth Circuit (*Runnebaum v. Nationsbank*, 123 F.3d 156, 1997) overturned a panel interpretation of the Americans with Disabilities Act (ADA). Runnebaum, a former employee of Nationsbank, brought a claim under the ADA arguing that his employer had terminated him as a result of an HIV infection. The original panel overturned the decision of the trial court to grant summary judgment, finding that an issue of material fact existed with regard to whether the employer regarded the employee as disabled and whether the reasons given for the termination were pretextual. Two of the original panel members were members of the "Democratic minority" in the circuit as a whole. The third member of the panel, a Republican, dissented from the majority opinion. After rehearing *en banc*, the majority opinion, authored by the dissenting member of the original panel, joined other Republican judges to vacate and reverse the panel's judgment. The Democrats on the original panel joined the other Democrats in the Fourth Circuit and one Ford appointee in dissent. Thus, the *en banc* procedure allowed the full circuit majority to overrule a panel whose policy preferences were contrary to those of the full circuit on an ideologically charged issue.

Jurisdictional Constraints

The U.S. Courts of Appeals have only appellate jurisdiction. They conduct no trials but instead are limited to reviewing the decisions of federal district courts and certain federal administrative agencies located within their geographic boundaries. Additional jurisdictional limits are imposed by Article 3 of the Constitution and enactments of Congress.

The jurisdiction of the circuit courts extends to appeals from both the civil and criminal law decisions of the district courts and some federal agencies. Perhaps most important, the courts of appeals may hear all appeals involving "federal questions." That is, the courts are empowered to hear cases that raise questions relating to the interpretation, application, or validity of federal laws and federal administrative regulations, the Constitution of the United States, and treaties of the United States. For example, any dispute in which either a state or national law is challenged as being contrary to the U.S. Constitution may be brought in federal district court and then appealed to the circuit courts. Similarly, the circuit courts are empowered to hear appeals of criminal defendants convicted of federal crimes[20] as well as appeals from district court decisions covering the broad spectrum of federal civil law (e.g., civil rights, antitrust, patents and copyrights, banking regulations, environmental and consumer protection, wage and hour restrictions, federal income tax, or farm subsidies).

The U.S. Courts of Appeals also may hear cases raising only substantive state law issues because the U.S. government is a party or the dispute involves citizens of different states ("diversity of citizenship"). For example, in a suit to recover damages from an accident involving a U.S. mail truck and a car driven by a private citizen, the case may be heard by federal courts even though the only substantive law to be applied will be the tort law of the state in which the accident occurred. Diversity jurisdiction extends to civil cases involving the laws of one or more states in which the defendant and plaintiff are citizens of different states. Beginning with the Judiciary Act of 1789, Congress has limited federal court jurisdiction to diversity actions in which the amount in question exceeded some minimum set by Congress. Initially set at $500 in 1789, the limit has been raised over time to the current requirement that the amount in question exceed $75,000. In both diversity cases and cases based on the role of the United States as a party to the litigation, federal judges hearing the case will be expected to apply the relevant state law, guided by the interpretation of the highest state court.[21] Finally, U.S. Courts of Appeals, like other federal courts, are empowered to decide several miscellaneous categories of cases that usually escape intensive public scrutiny. Among these categories of federal jurisdiction are disputes involving the ambassadors of foreign countries and admiralty law cases.

Policy-Making by the Courts of Appeals

When considered from a functional perspective, the U.S. Courts of Appeals play three major roles. First, they are charged with "error correction." The right of all losing parties in the district courts and administrative agencies to a mandatory review on demand guarantees that the circuit courts will have a chance to review all decisions in which one of the parties feels strongly that a miscarriage of justice occurred. The courts of appeals are charged with the duty to examine such claims carefully and to redress any misinterpretation of law or egregious errors in fact-finding by the trial court. In the role of error correction, the emphasis is to settle justly the concrete dispute between the litigants regardless of whether or not it has any policy implications for a wider audience. The courts of appeals are also called upon to settle a number of cases in which there is little doubt about the correctness of the decision below. Richardson and Vines (1970, 118) note that appeals court dockets contain "ritualistic appeals" in which lawyers representing politically oriented clients in "cause" litigation (e.g., a civil rights case) may pursue an appeal they realize has little chance of success simply to demonstrate their commitment to the cause, as well as "frivolous appeals" that lack any serious legal merit brought by prisoners or others who have nothing to lose. The role of the courts of appeals in such cases is primarily one of legitimizing the process and reinforcing beliefs in the fairness and justice of the legal system. Finally, the courts of appeals hear a number of cases every year that give them an opportunity to act as policymakers. Since the policy-making role of the Supreme Court is severely limited by the tiny portion of federal cases that it can hear,[22] much of the development of precedent and the shaping of legal policy is left to the courts of appeals.

The role that the courts play in the making of public policy is enhanced by the nature of their business. The business of the courts of appeals has changed dramatically over the past century. The most obvious change has been the dramatic increase in the sheer volume of cases, especially in the past two decades. As can be seen from figure 1.2 and the summary of that data in table 1.2, the caseload of the courts of appeals remained relatively stable from the passage of the Judges Bill in 1925 until the early 1960s when the number of cases exploded. After rising slowly from 1891 to 3,500 appeals in 1936, the court's caseload declined slightly and did not reach 3,500 cases again until 1957. Then, from 1960 to 1967, the number of cases more than doubled to over 7,700. In the next six years it doubled again to over 15,000 cases in 1973. Since 1973 the flood has continued, although at a slightly slower rate of increase, reaching 23,155 cases by 1980 and 37,524 in 1988. Cumulatively, there has been close to a fifteenfold increase in the number of cases before the circuit courts since 1925 and almost a tenfold increase since 1960.

Consideration of the nature of the cases heard by the U.S. Courts of Appeals suggests the potential for substantial impact on the formation and implementation of public policy. Substantial numbers of cases directly deal with questions of public law, especially those dealing with the enforcement of criminal law, the treatment and rights of prisoners, civil rights issues including claims of race, sex, and age discrimination, the distribution of government benefits, taxation, and government regulation of economic activity. More than 70 percent of all the cases directly involve some level of government, most frequently the national government. While some of these cases appear to represent little more than the routine affirmance of

TABLE 1.2.   The Increasing Caseload of
the U.S. Courts of Appeals

Year	Cases[a]
1925	2,525
1930	2,874
1935	3,514
1940	3,446
1945	2,730
1950	2,678
1955	3,544
1960	3,765
1965	6,597
1970	11,440
1975	16,571
1980	23,155
1985	33,360
1988	37,524

Source: Annual Reports of the Administrative Office
of the United States Courts.
[a]Total number of cases filed in fiscal year

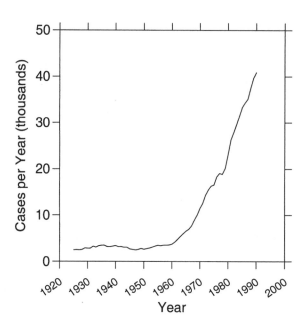

FIG. 1.2.   The caseload explosion

the denial by the district court of some benefit or claim of a procedural irregularity in an individual case with no clear significance to anyone other than the aggrieved party, many result in opinions that spend pages explaining the meaning of statutory (or, less frequently, constitutional) rules in terms that on their face appear to shape the meaning of the law for the broader public.

The Final Forum

The U.S. Courts of Appeals are important policymakers not only because they hear issues that have important political consequences, but because in the resolution of those issues they are the final forum for the resolution of most disputes over the meaning of federal law. In theory, all decisions of the courts of appeals are reviewable by the Supreme Court. If the High Court actually did review a large percentage of their decisions then the role of the courts of appeals in policy-making would be slight. But a basic condition of our judicial system is that the Supreme Court exerts very little direct supervision over any of the lower courts (Howard 1981, 57).

The first factor that increases appeals court autonomy is that most litigants who lose do not seek Supreme Court review. Appeals court independence is further enhanced by the infrequency with which petitions for review are granted. In a leading study of federal appellate litigation decided by three circuits during the period 1965 through 1968, Howard (1981) found that only 20 percent of the losing litigants in the courts of appeals petitioned for certiorari. In addition, his results indicated that the Court gave full review to only 1.3 percent of the cases decided by the courts of appeals.

In the twenty years since the period studied by Howard, the caseload of the courts of appeals has increased dramatically, but the number of decisions handed down each year by the Supreme Court has remained relatively constant. As a result, it might be expected that the proportion of appeals court decisions reviewed by the Supreme Court has declined even below the already low rates noted by Howard. Recent research (Songer 1991) confirms this expectation. Analysis of the decisions of three circuits in 1986 revealed that the Supreme Court reviewed only 19 of the nearly 4,000 decisions—a rate of review under one-half of one percent. Of those accepted for review, the Supreme Court reversed the decision below about two-thirds of the time. But since so few cases were reviewed at all, the net result was that the decision of the court of appeals was left undisturbed in 99.7 percent of their cases. Even when attention is confined to the more important policy-making decisions of the courts of appeals, the picture is similar. Our analysis of a sample of 1,080 cases that resulted in a published decision in the period 1986 through 1988 found only 1.7 percent of the appeals courts' policy pronouncements were reviewed by the Supreme Court.

The net result is broad autonomy for the U.S. Courts of Appeals. In some areas, such as diversity of citizenship cases, the Supreme Court has in effect delegated the role of final appellate decision maker to the courts of appeals. In a few selected areas, most notably civil rights in recent years, the Supreme Court maintains an active interest and devotes a substantial portion of its docket to reviewing the decisions of the courts of appeals. Yet even in these areas, the overwhelming majority of appeals court decisions are left undisturbed, even when the policy interests supported below seem to be contrary to the general thrust of Supreme Court preferences. Therefore, thousands of appeals court decisions each year establish circuit precedent in policy areas where Supreme Court attention is sporadic. Moreover, the objective odds that any given decision will be reviewed are so low that it seems safe to assume that the consequences of review are not likely to weigh heavily on the minds of the appeals court decision makers.

Judicial Oversight of Administrative Agencies

A sometimes overlooked, but critical task of the courts of appeals is their role in providing judicial oversight of federal administrative agencies. For decades, students of American politics have recognized that administrative agencies are important political actors. As Peters notes, federal administrative agencies are "major formulators" of policy (1989). Central to their role as policymakers is the extensive discretion exercised by administrative agencies (Horowitz 1994). While there is widespread acceptance of the necessity for administrative discretion, a normative consensus exists that such discretion should be constrained by administrative deference to the policy preferences of the president and Congress in addition to the substantive and procedural requirements of the rule of law. It is well known, however, that neither subservience to their political superiors nor fidelity to the rule of law can be assumed to characterize all administrative action. Anecdotal evidence abounds of the abuse of discretion that results in the interjection of personal favoritism or political bias into administrative decisions. "Discretion has its dark side . . . [it] enables and even invites officials to overreach, to discriminate invidiously, to subordinate public interests to private ones . . . and to tyrannize over the citizenry" (Schuck 1994, 155). As a result, control of administrative discretion has been a "central problem" for both theorists and practitioners of politics in the United States (Horowitz 1994). In this context, judicial review is seen as a "check on lawlessness, a check on administrative agents making choices based on convenient personal or political preferences without substantial concern for matters of inconvenient principle" (Robinson 1991, 181). The courts of appeals have traditionally played a central role in the judicial review of agency decisions. Appeals of many agency decisions go directly to the courts of appeals without the necessity of any prior action by the district courts. For the remainder of agency decisions that are first reviewed by the district courts, the courts of appeals usually provide the final review.[23] The role of the courts of appeals is particularly important when the primary issue is whether or not the agency has abused its discretion. This traditional appeals court role of supervising administrative agencies has steadily grown in importance over the last several decades in response to the expanding caseloads and decreasing rates of review by the Supreme Court noted above. As a result, the courts of appeals have become the final arbiter in practice for the overwhelming majority of challenges to the decisions of federal administrative agencies (Songer 1991). Therefore, if there is to be any legal check on abuse of discretion by administrative agencies, the courts of appeals are likely to play a crucial role.

Framework of Analysis

As the preceding review of scholarship indicates, the courts of appeals are clearly established as important policymakers in the American federal system. Their agenda now spans a broad array of issues that includes many of the most important and controversial concerns of domestic politics. But in spite of our growing understanding of the policy-making role of the courts of appeals, many questions remain unanswered. There is a critical need for good longitudinal studies that span significant time periods. We know little about how changes over time in the social, economic, and political context may be related to judicial decision making and the types of issues and litigants that are on the courts' dockets. Additionally, while recent scholarship has provided some answers to the question of who wins and who loses in contemporary federal courts, we know little about whether these patterns reflect recent developments or long-standing trends in the judiciary.

The main thrust of the analysis of this book is to investigate the extent of continuity and change in the U.S. Courts of Appeals over a major portion of the twentieth century. Our analysis starts with a critical juncture in court history, the passage of the "Judges Bill" in 1925, which completed the codification of federal appellate jurisdiction and set up the basic scheme of organization that persists to this day for the federal courts (Richardson and Vines 1970). The analysis examines changes and similarities in the types of people recruited to serve on the federal bench, traces the development of the agenda of the courts of appeals, identifies the winners and losers at each period, and examines the evolution of judicial decision making over a sixty-four-year span. In the broadest sense, we seek to discover whether what we as social scientists "know" about the federal courts from the studies of the past two or three decades stands up under an analysis of data that spans over six decades.

To facilitate the analysis of change over time, the sixty-four years of data included in the Courts of Appeals Data Base were divided into five periods. The periods capture significant changes in the legal and political history of the twentieth century that might plausibly affect the likelihood of success by underdogs. In the first period, 1925 through 1936, the legal system was dominated by conservative, pro-business judges at all levels of the judicial system. Our second period, 1937 through 1945, begins with the "switch in time that saved nine" which marked the beginning of the Roosevelt Court and its aggressive pro–New Deal policies. Throughout this period, the courts came to be dominated by Roosevelt judges who were selected in large part for their devotion to New Deal economic policies that had a decidedly pro-underdog orientation (Goldman 1997). The third period, 1946 through 1960, was characterized by a return to moderation, with both Truman and Eisenhower appointees to the lower courts being selected without much regard for their policy preferences. The fourth period, 1961 through 1969, was most notable for the leadership of the judiciary by the Warren Court, perhaps the most liberal Court in our history, particularly in issues related to criminal law and procedure. This period also was characterized by two Democratic presidential administrations, dramatic agitation in Congress and on the streets for expansion of civil rights, and advocacy for the welfare of poor people that culminated in President Johnson's War on Poverty. During our final period, 1970 through 1988, the only Democratic president, Jimmy Carter, did not have an opportunity to make any Supreme Court appointments. As a result, the Supreme Court became steadily more conservative as the appointees of Nixon, Ford, and Reagan ascended to the high bench. However, during the same period, President Carter had an opportunity to make a major impact on the courts of appeals by appointing fifty-six judges to new positions and to vacancies.

Data Sources and the Organization of the Analysis

This manuscript provides the first detailed analysis of the United States Courts of Appeals Data Base, the richest and largest data base ever assembled for the study of American courts. After a six-year development period, the data base was archived at the ICPSR in early 1998. With the guidance of the advisory board, a revised proposal was funded by the National Science Foundation for the creation of a multiuser data base consisting of data from a substantial sample of published decisions from 1925 to 1988. The data base involved the coding of a random sample of decisions from each circuit for each year for the period 1925–88. The total size of this sample is 15,315 decisions. A more detailed description of the data base is provided in the appendix.

The analysis below is summarized in four substantive chapters. The second chapter opens with a discussion of the judicial selection process that gives attention to both the formal process as well as the political criteria that guide presidential choice and the practical constraints imposed by the necessity of senatorial courtesy. An overview of the types of people who secure appointment to the courts of appeals demonstrates elements of both continuity and change over time. Examination of changes in the demographic composition of the courts shows the increasing diversity in terms of race, gender, and religion and how the changing priorities of recent presidents have helped to diversify the courts. In particular, this chapter notes the impact of the merit selection system created by President Carter and the increased politicization of the process by Reagan on both the diversity of the bench and on indicators of the professionalization of the bench.

The third chapter provides a detailed analysis of the changing agenda of the courts over time and the continuing wide variation in the nature of the issues brought before different circuits. These trends are examined within the framework of social development theory and the contributions of the political, legal, and institutional contexts to changing agendas. The analysis indicates that agenda changes have been substantial. Prisoner petitions and civil liberties decisions have increased dramatically, with judicial attention to criminal appeals, after experiencing considerable growth in the 1960s and 1970s, now appearing to have leveled off. In addition to the discovery of common trends across time, differences among circuits remain substantial, in contrast to the conventional view that nationalizing forces have produced convergence among the circuits.

The fourth chapter builds on the earlier work of Sheehan and Songer that suggested the wide disparity in litigant resources among the parties appearing before the courts of appeals to be substantially related to who won and who lost. Contrary to the myth of equality before the law, judicial scholars have found that in recent years those that have access to money and organizational resources fare much better than individuals who are one-shot players in the lower courts. This chapter extends their line of research by examining change over time to determine whether political and structural changes (e.g., the rise of legal aid societies and changing legal doctrine governing rules on access) enhance or mitigate the advantages enjoyed by the "haves" in the courts of appeals.

In the final substantive chapter, the decisional tendencies of the judges are examined over time. Prior studies indicate that, for appeals court judges, party affiliation and regional origins are consistent predictors of judicial voting. However, these prior studies have relied on data from the recent past. From 1925 to 1988 (the period covered by the Appeals Court Data Base), the nature of the party system and the meaning of regionalism in society at large has changed dramatically. The fifth chapter provides an initial look at how changes in partisanship and region in the larger political system are related to changes in the decisional trends of appeals court judges. The longitudinal analysis clearly indicates that findings based on recent decisions of appeals court judges may not be generalized over time. As detailed in this later chapter, partisanship has become more pronounced in recent years whereas the significance of region for appeals court decision making has declined sharply.

CHAPTER 2

A Profile of Judges on the U.S. Courts of Appeals

The policy outputs of any court depend on its membership; therefore, our analysis begins by profiling the men and women who staffed the circuit courts from 1925 to 1988. Since judges do not select themselves, this analysis focuses on the links between paths to the bench and judicial attributes. As J. Woodford Howard noted in his 1981 work on these courts, "to understand how judges reach courts of appeals is to dissect long-term interaction between professional development and political recruitment" (90). Although he concluded that the backgrounds of judges sitting on three circuits in the 1960s tended to be similar, other research suggests that there may be some subtle differences and that these differences may be attributed to the selection procedures and constraints faced by appointing presidents (Goldman 1997; Slotnick 1988). In this chapter, we examine longitudinal and geographical trends in demographic, professional, and political characteristics of judges on the courts of appeals within a context that recognizes the consequences of recruitment processes associated with various presidential administrations. We initially investigate the linkages between the selection process and the partisan balance of the appeals court bench and then compare the varying paths to the bench over time, including political and legal backgrounds. In addition to these characteristics, we present data on the demographic attributes of these judges. Finally, we turn to institutional and geographically based influences on the staffing of the bench. Here, we explore the potential for forum shopping as the staffing of judges may vary by circuit, thus providing litigants an opportunity to pursue their case in a circuit more favorably disposed to their position.

Presidents and Judicial Selection

The Constitution provides for presidential appointment of judges with the advice and consent of the Senate. Through their appointments, presidents may affect policy-making long after their tenure in office. However, one constraint on presidential influence concerns the number of opportunities to make appointments. Such opportunities arise either when judges leave office (as a result of retirement or death) or when a new seat is created by legislative enactment. Not surprisingly, the timing of judicial vacancies does not appear to be random. Recent research by Barrow, Zuk, and Gryski (1996) indicates federal judges have been more likely to leave when the current administration is governed by their party. Relatedly, their study also found the creation of judicial posts to be strategically timed, as omnibus judges bills were more likely to be enacted when the president's party held a majority in Congress. The data presented in figure 2.1 support that interpretation. For example, following President Carter's inauguration in 1977, there were 92 appeals court judges. By 1980, after the passage of an omnibus judges bill by Congress, the number of judges in the lower federal appellate courts had swelled to 120.

The selection processes adopted by each administration can vary with the weight given to criteria in the appointment process (Goldman 1997). From this perspective, an administration can undertake a deliberate effort to appoint judges who will advance, through their decisions, the policy agenda of the president. Other administrations may utilize judicial appointments for partisan goals. In this respect, presidents view judicial appointments as vehicles for advancing their own political base or the stature of their parties. Some presidents, on occasion, use judicial appointments as opportunities for rewarding close friends who have been loyal throughout their political career. Selection processes also vary by administration in terms of the personal involvement of the president and the attention given to input by home-state senators and others interested in the staffing of the bench. As detailed below, judicial selection strategies ultimately may shape the profile of those selected to staff the bench.

Over time, the process of appointing men and women to the U.S. Courts of Appeals has shifted with changes in presidential administrations. Judges sitting on the bench in the earlier years (1925–36) were selected by presidents who utilized varying selection strategies. President Teddy Roosevelt was perhaps the first to recognize the connection between policy goals and judicial appointments (Solomon 1984). In the last years of his administration, officials scrutinized candidates' views on labor and antitrust issues. Similarly, President Wilson also utilized a judicial selection strategy that focused on the policy views of nominees to the U.S. Courts of Appeals. In contrast, Presidents Taft and Hoover adopted appointment

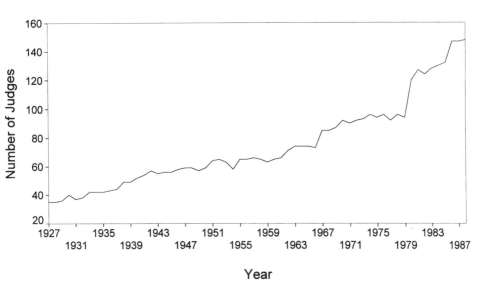

FIG. 2.1.   Judges of the U.S. Courts of Appeals. (Data from Data Base on Attributes of U.S. Appeals Court Judges, NSF Grant #SBR-93–11999.)

processes that valued professionalism (Solomon 1984). Finally, Presidents Harding and Coolidge viewed appointments to the U.S. Courts of Appeals as opportunities to curry favor with individual senators in the Senate (Solomon 1984).

During the tenure of Franklin Roosevelt in the period preceding and including World War II (1937–45), judicial selection in the lower courts again was transformed. In the early years of the administration, Roosevelt officials utilized appointments to advance partisan goals (Goldman 1997). However, after 1937, administration officials frequently sought judicial candidates whose policy views were supportive of the goals of the New Deal (Goldman 1997; Solomon 1984). Rather than relying on senators to recommend appointees, Justice Department officials began taking the initiative in identifying a nominee with a "favorable" judicial temperament. Some senators even appeared to respond to the changing criteria. In a speech on behalf of a nominee to the U.S. Courts of Appeals, one senator recited cases in which the nominee (a sitting district court judge) had upheld New Deal legislation (Solomon 1984, 327). Not surprisingly, one scholar found that references to policy views appeared in 57 percent of Department of Justice files on appeals court judges appointed by FDR between 1935 and 1940 (Goldman 1997).

With precedent in economic policy well-established by Roosevelt judges, officials in the Truman administration frequently utilized appointments as rewards for political loyalty to the president (Goldman 1997). Although Truman's personal-agenda appointments to the Supreme Court are well-known, he also remembered other friends with appointments to the lower courts, such as Caskie Collet, a Missourian named to the Eighth Circuit. Like his predecessor, Eisenhower did not closely scrutinize policy views. However, this Republican administration, like several earlier ones, placed an emphasis on the qualifications of nominees (Goldman 1997). Although Eisenhower and Truman utilized differing criteria in their appointment process, both men turned to the ranks of their respective parties for nominees (Goldman 1997).

The domination of the White House and Congress by Democrats through most of the 1960s also affected the lower court judicial appointment process. The norm of senatorial courtesy[1] and the power of Senate Judiciary Committee chair James Eastland (D-MS) forced administration officials to adopt strategies for judicial selection that would include input from Democratic supporters in Congress. Several accounts of judicial nominations made during the Kennedy Administration document instances where officials recognized that appointments could be used to support the president in congressional relations (McFeeley 1987; Navasky 1971). Kennedy officials made a special effort to avoid confrontations with southern legislators over judicial appointments, particularly those to the trial court bench. As former majority leader, Johnson also recognized the political capital associated with appointments to the lower federal courts and frequently took a personal interest in the appointments to the lower courts (McFeeley 1987). Johnson did not ignore completely the views of the nominees. In a correspondence with then–deputy attorney general Ramsey Clark, Johnson noted, "check to be sure he [the prospective nominee] is all right on the civil rights question. I'll approve him if he is" (McFeeley 1987, 43).

The return of a Republican to the White House in 1969 again shifted the process of judicial selection. President Nixon strongly supported restoring "law and order" to the criminal justice system. With his U.S. Supreme Court appointments, Nixon clearly affected the doctrinal trends in claims involving the rights of criminal defendants. Although many believed that the law-and-order perspective was necessary to be appointed to the lower court, Nixon was not particularly interested in lower court judicial selection, and, as a result, there was relatively little effort undertaken to screen nominees on their views (Goldman 1997). In general, Nixon delegated much of the responsibility for lower court judicial appointments to John Ehrlichman (Goldman 1997). Nixon's rhetoric recognized the potential connection between policy goals and appointments, but in practice, appointments appeared to advance partisan goals (Goldman 1997). In the aftermath of Watergate, President Ford inherited an administration and its judicial selection procedures. Facing enormous political problems associated with the integrity of the presidency and the Republican Party, Ford replaced administration officials responsible for judicial selection with individuals who tended to be "non political types" (Goldman 1989a).

In the late 1970s, Democrats returned to the White House with the election of Jimmy Carter, who promised to institute a "merit selection" procedure for the appointment of federal judges while adopting a policy of affirmative action as a means of bringing diversity to the staffing of the federal judiciary (Fowler 1984). Following his election, Carter established commissions within each circuit to identify potential nominees for vacancies on the U.S. Courts of Appeals. His subsequent appointments resulted in a cohort that included a record number of minorities and women (Goldman 1997). However, the policy views and partisan background of nominees were not overlooked. The makeup of the commissions included Democratic Party activists with the "final" recommendation for an appointment coming from the attorney general and officials in the White House, including congressional liaison staff member Frank More, Jody Powell, Hamilton Jordan, and White House counsel Robert Lipshutz (Goldman 1997; Slotnick 1988). Carter's agenda for judicial appointments placed an emphasis on identifying qualified minorities and women; however, the White House also was interested in other goals, including those advancing partisan and policy concerns. In contrast to approaches taken by his Democratic predecessors in the 1960s, Carter's use of commissions and affirmative action policy minimized the influence of individual Democratic senators in the selection of U.S. Courts of Appeals judges. Moreover, the creation of numerous vacancies through judges bills gave President Carter more leverage to name the administration's preferred candidate to the bench.

The election of Ronald Reagan in 1980 led to fundamental changes in judicial selection for the lower courts by institutionalizing the central role played by White House advisers in the identification of nominees and establishing selection procedures that centered on the recruitment of those with specific policy views (Fowler 1984). The most prominent figure in judicial selection throughout the Reagan administration, Edwin Meese, called for the appointment of judges who would exercise greater restraint and emphasize "original intent" (Goldman 1989b). Meese named a special assistant to the Justice Department whose responsibilities included studying the judicial philosophy of potential nominees to the federal bench (Goldman 1997). Judicial candidates were interviewed on a variety of topics, including their positions on legal policy issues, to an unprecedented degree. As documented in one account, a candidate to the appeals court bench had all of his previously published decisions as a district court judge analyzed by Department of Justice officials who were concerned about the nominee's philosophy (Goldman 1997, 306).

Like President Carter, Reagan's selection procedures tended to minimize the input of individual senators. In his first term, the advice-and-consent role of the Senate was marked by cooperation, particularly from conservative Republicans. In Reagan's second term, however, controversy surrounded several nominations as interest groups began to participate actively in the confirmation process. In the past, confirmation of a lower federal court judge was low profile with a voice vote that was generally unanimous. However, during the last two years of the Reagan administration, Democrats regained a majority in the Senate, and interest groups mobilized their efforts so that three nominations to the appeals court bench were vigorously debated with roll-call votes on confirmation (Goldman 1997).

In summary, the description of the selection procedures adopted by presidents offers several insights for the purposes of this analysis. To begin with, Democratic and Republican presidents generally have adopted lower-court judicial selection procedures that are markedly different. Constrained by powerful senators of their own party, Democratic presidents more frequently have focused on partisan goals in their appointments.[2] As a result, one would expect Democratic appointees to be more closely tied to political concerns associated with home-state senators than Republican appointees are. In contrast, most Republican presidents have served during divided government (with fewer home-state senators of their party), which gives them more latitude with judicial appointments to the lower courts as the norm of senatorial courtesy generally will not apply. Dealing with a Democratic Congress, however, also may lead Republican presidents to make a few more cross-party appointments. A second consideration highlighted above is that Republican presidents, particularly those in earlier years, placed greater emphasis on the qualifications of their appointees. Therefore, one would expect Republican appointees to have had more extensive judicial and legal experience than their Democratic counterparts (particularly during the presidencies of Eisenhower, Taft, and Hoover). Finally, the appointees of Democratic and Republican presidents should be similar in their social backgrounds, since judges of both parties represent an elite; however, to the extent that differences exist, they should reflect their parties' constituencies. For this reason, Democratic presidents would be more likely to appoint "nontraditional" nominees than Republican presidents.

From a longitudinal perspective, changes in judicial selection over time also should influence the characteristics of those appointed. With increased presidential involvement, other political actors, including interest groups and congressional leaders, have more closely scrutinized nominees (Hartley and Holmes 1997). One would expect that, in recent years, presidents of both parties would attempt to deflect criticism by appointing judges who have had more extensive and prestigious legal backgrounds. Finally, changes in the legal profession that parallel broader social change also may contribute to changes in judicial backgrounds. Increasingly, lawyers have become more diverse in terms of their social backgrounds. Like other professionals, lawyers have become more mobile, leading one to anticipate that judicial backgrounds would include more varied career experiences over time.

Presidential Appointments and the Partisan Balance of the Bench

To initially assess the backgrounds of judges on the U.S. Courts of Appeals, we examine the partisan balance of the bench over time. In the data presented in figure 2.2, the percentage of the bench staffed by judges appointed by Democratic presidents rises and falls over time with rises occurring at a slight lag after the election of a Democratic president and falls at a slight lag after the election of a Republican president. As the chart demonstrates, the impact of a president's judicial appointments may be felt long after the tenure of the administration. In addition, strategically timed judges bills can have long-term effects on the ideological makeup of the bench. For example, the influx of new judicial seats occupied by Carter appointees contributed to a more evenly balanced bench during the 1980s

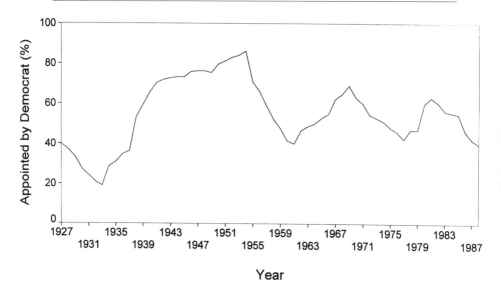

FIG. 2.2.   U.S. Appeals Court bench, by year. (Data from Data Base on Attributes of U.S. Appeals Court Judges, NSF Grant #SBR-93–11999.)

when Republican presidents occupied the White House. We examine more specifically the impact of the appointments of individual presidents in table 2.1.

Table 2.1 presents the distribution, by appointing president, of judges on the courts of appeals over time. As these data suggest, some presidents, by virtue of their longevity or the well-timed passage of judges bills, were able to appoint a significant number of judges. Shifts in the partisan balance of the courts reflect on these political dynamics. In the first period (1925–36), Republican presidents' appointees were in the majority, yet the partisan difference between judges was relatively small. However, with the election of Roosevelt in 1932, the bench became overwhelmingly Democratic. In the third period (1946–60), Eisenhower appointees restored partisan balance in the staffing of the U.S. Courts of Appeals. Yet again, the Kennedy-Johnson terms in the 1960s led to a bench dominated by Democrats. In the last period examined (1970–88), Republican judges were in the majority, with the election of only one Democratic president during the 1970s and 1980s. Overall, judges appointed by Republican presidents made

TABLE 2.1. U.S. Courts of Appeals Judges' Party Affiliation and Appointing President, by Time Period (in percentages)

Judicial Attribute	Period 1 (1925–36)	Period 2 (1937–45)	Period 3 (1946–60)	Period 4 (1961–69)	Period 5 (1970–88)
Party Affiliation					
Democratic	54.4	74.2	45.6	74.8	39.5
	($n = 43$)	($n = 46$)	($n = 47$)	($n = 83$)	($n = 107$)
Republican	45.6	25.8	54.4	24.3	57.9
	($n = 36$)	($n = 16$)	($n = 56$)	($n = 27$)	($n = 157$)
Independent					1.8
					($n = 5$)
Other				0.9	0.8
				($n = 1$)	($n = 2$)
Appointing President					
Harrison	2.5				
	($n = 2$)				
Cleveland	1.3				
	($n = 1$)				
McKinley	1.3				
	($n = 1$)				
T. Roosevelt	5.1	4.8			
	($n = 4$)	($n = 3$)			
Taft	5.1	1.6			
	($n = 4$)	($n = 1$)			
Wilson	21.5	6.5	1.9		
	($n = 17$)	($n = 4$)	($n = 2$)		
Harding	6.3				
	($n = 5$)				
Coolidge	21.5	6.5	5.8		
	($n = 17$)	($n = 4$)	($n = 6$)		
Hoover	20.3	9.7	6.8	0.9	
	($n = 16$)	($n = 6$)	($n = 7$)	($n = 1$)	
F. D. Roosevelt	15.2	61.3	20.4	10.8	0.4
	($n = 12$)	($n = 38$)	($n = 21$)	($n = 12$)	($n = 1$)
Truman		9.7	22.3	10.8	0.7
		($n = 6$)	($n = 23$)	($n = 12$)	($n = 2$)
Eisenhower			42.7	13.5	8.5
			($n = 44$)	($n = 15$)	($n = 23$)
Kennedy				17.1	5.5
				($n = 19$)	($n = 15$)
Johnson				36.9	14.8
				($n = 41$)	($n = 40$)
Nixon				9.9	16.6
				($n = 11$)	($n = 45$)
Ford					4.4
					($n = 12$)
Carter					20.7
					($n = 56$)
Reagan					28.4
					($n = 77$)
Number of Judges on the Bench	79	62	103	111	271

up a majority of those on the bench in the first (1925–36), third (1946–60), and fifth (1970–88) periods. In the second (1937–45) and fourth (1961–69) periods, the ratio of sitting judges appointed by Democratic presidents to those appointed by Republicans was nearly three to one.

The data in table 2.1 also indicate how the subsequent tables should be interpreted. The characteristics of judges in each period reflect not simply those appointed during that period, but all sitting judges during that time period. For example, some judges appointed by FDR are included in a cohort across several time periods. The cohorts presented in the later tables, divided by time periods, are defined according to the party of the appointing president.

Judicial Nominations

Before profiling judicial backgrounds, we examine in table 2.2 the characteristics surrounding the appointment process of judges on the U.S. Courts of Appeals. Nominations associated with newly created seats on the U.S. Courts of Appeals should not be subject to the same constraints stemming from the Senate's advise-and-consent role when compared to those where the nominee replaces a judge who had left the bench. With the exception of those seats established with reorganization in the early years of the U.S. Courts of Appeals, the number of new seats has risen over time with the creation of judicial vacancies generally benefiting Democratic presidents. On the other hand, this table indicates that Democratic presidents likely faced greater constraints in the nomination process, with nearly three-fourths of all appointees coming from states represented by Democratic senators. In particular, the table suggests that Presidents Kennedy and Johnson faced more constraints than their immediate predecessor (Eisenhower) and successor (Nixon), respectively. These aggregate data are supported by scholarly accounts of individual nominations as well. In one instance, Kennedy officials were pressured by Senator John McClellan (D-AR) to name a former adviser to segregationist Governor Faubus to a seat on the Eighth Circuit. Administration officials initially resisted the pressure of Senator McClellan but capitulated when the senator made it apparent that he would block any other nomination put forward to fill this vacancy (Goldman 1997).

These data also indicate that judges on the U.S. Courts of Appeals who did not share the party of their appointing president have been relatively few in number. Of the varying cohorts examined, Republican presidents

TABLE 2.2. Characteristics of U.S. Courts of Appeals Judges' Appointments, by Presidential Party and Time Period (in percentages)

Characteristic of Nomination	Period 1 (1925–36) Dem. Pres. (n = 30)	Period 1 (1925–36) Rep. Pres. (n = 49)	Period 2 (1937–45) Dem. Pres. (n = 48)	Period 2 (1937–45) Rep. Pres. (n = 14)	Period 3 (1946–60) Dem. Pres. (n = 46)	Period 3 (1946–60) Rep. Pres. (n = 57)	Period 4 (1961–69) Dem. Pres. (n = 84)	Period 4 (1961–69) Rep. Pres. (n = 27)	Period 5 (1970–88) Dem. Pres. (n = 114)	Period 5 (1970–88) Rep. Pres. (n = 157)
Appointee to fill new seat	6.7	34.7	27.1	35.7	13.0	12.3	18.6	29.6	45.6	20.4
Home-state senator of presidential party in office	76.7	71.4	70.8	57.1	80.4	63.2	72.6	51.9	78.1	70.1
ABA Rating of Well qualified and above	—	—	—	—	0	70.5	60.3	88.5	69.9	64.3
Cross party appointment	3.3	14.3	6.3	7.1	8.7	8.8	3.6	7.4	10.5	4.4

Note: ABA ratings were first utilized in the third period (1946–60) during the Eisenhower administration. During this time, ABA ratings are available for only 63 judges. In the fourth period, ratings are available for 94 judges, and in the fifth period, for 270 judges.

from the early twentieth century were more likely to appoint judges from the opposing party. This finding is not particularly surprising, as presidents Taft and Hoover emphasized criteria that were not related to policy or partisan concerns.[3] Over time, however, the likelihood of a Republican appointing a Democrat appears to have fallen. In contrast, cross-party appointments of Democratic presidents have varied, reflecting on their strategy in judicial selection. The percentage of cross-party appointments sitting on the bench during the post–World War II period reflects an upward trend. Truman's appointments, who generally sat on the bench during the postwar period, were selected through a process that recognized the partisan and personal value of appointments, at times during periods of divided government. In contrast, Democratic presidents Kennedy and Johnson often utilized appointments to advance their stature vis-à-vis a Democratic Congress. Not surprisingly, nearly all judges appointed by Democratic presidents and sitting on the bench during the 1960s also tended to be Democrats. This trend shifted with the initiation of merit judicial selection procedures under President Carter. The ability of President Carter to turn to nominees outside the party also was facilitated by the creation of new seats on the bench that had not yet been tied to the interests of particular states.

During the appointment process, the judicial qualities of prospective nominees are rated by the American Bar Association Standing Committee on Federal Judiciary. The ratings were initially utilized by President Eisenhower, who was clearly concerned that his appointees be well-qualified. Not surprisingly, the Eisenhower cohort had the highest percentage of appeals court judges who were rated as well-qualified (or exceptionally well-qualified). Research conducted to assess what determines ABA ratings has not found any relationship between the nominee's political activity and their ABA rating (Slotnick 1983). However, higher ABA ratings have generally gone to those nominees with more bar experience so that more "traditional candidates" tend to rate higher than those nominees who followed a nontraditional path to the bench (Slotnick 1983). In recent years, officials in the Carter and Reagan administrations continued to utilize ABA ratings but would still pursue some nominations where candidates received a "not qualified" ABA rating (Goldman 1997).

Paths to the Bench

The paths to the bench for judges of the U.S. Courts of Appeals have varied over time and by party of the appointing president (see table 2.3). In the

TABLE 2.3. U.S. Courts of Appeals Judges' Paths to the Bench (in percentages)

	Period 1 (1925–36)		Period 2 (1937–45)		Period 3 (1946–60)		Period 4 (1961–69)		Period 5 (1970–88)	
	Dem. Pres. (n = 30)	Rep. Pres. (n = 49)	Dem. Pres. (n = 48)	Rep. Pres. (n = 14)	Dem. Pres. (n = 46)	Rep. Pres. (n = 57)	Dem. Pres. (n = 84)	Rep. Pres. (n = 27)	Dem. Pres. (n = 114)	Rep. Pres. (n = 157)
Median number of positions prior to appointment	4	4	4	3	4	3	4	3	4	4
Position held at time of appointment										
Dist. Ct. Judge	26.7	61.2	31.3	42.9	34.8	45.6	39.3	48.1	34.2	43.9
State Ct. Judge	20.0	10.2	16.7	14.3	6.5	12.3	11.9	—	15.8	10.2
Priv. Practice	20.0	6.1	20.8	—	21.7	21.1	29.8	37.0	30.7	28.0
First position held										
Priv. Practice	80.0	77.6	70.8	85.7	78.3	70.2	52.4	74.1	64.0	67.5
State prosec.	6.7	16.3	6.3	7.1	2.2	15.8	2.4	7.4	5.3	5.1
Law prof.	3.3	—	8.3	—	2.2	3.5	1.2	—	3.5	2.5
Clerk for fed. judge	—	—	4.2	—	2.2	3.5	1.2	—	10.5	12.7

early years (1925–36), the overwhelming majority of sitting judges appointed by Republican presidents were elevated from the federal district court. Of those elevated by Republican presidents, about one-third had only one type of career experience prior to their federal court appointment: private practice. In contrast, judges sitting on the bench who were appointed by Democratic presidents in the early years were selected from various positions, including federal district court, state courts, and private practice. In the second period, judicial selection by Franklin Roosevelt did not yield judges with substantially different paths to the bench. Most judges, regardless of the party of the appointing president, tended to begin their careers in private practice. Interestingly, Roosevelt's judicial selection procedures included the recruitment of a few judges whose careers began with clerkships in federal courts or with appointments to law schools.

The career paths of judges sitting on the bench in the post–World War II era begin to evidence fewer differences across cohorts. One of the few remaining differences is that appointees of Republican presidents included more individuals who began their careers as prosecutors in state court. Partisan differences in paths to the bench for judges sitting on the bench in the 1960s were similar to those identified in the second, earlier period of domination by Democratic presidents (1937–45). About 12 percent of judges appointed by Democratic presidents were sitting on a state court at the time of selection whereas none of the sitting judges appointed by Republican presidents held a state court position at the time of appointment.

In the most recent period, the paths to the bench look remarkably similar across presidential appointment cohorts. Interestingly, two paths to the bench that were relatively infrequent in earlier years have emerged. In one path, several judges began their career on the faculty of a law school. A second, increasingly "popular" path includes clerking in federal court. About one-tenth of all judges sitting on the bench from 1970 through 1988 clerked for a federal judge.

Political Careers

The data presented in table 2.4 provide more detail on the political backgrounds of judges on the U.S. Courts of Appeals. As we have suggested, judges selected by Republican presidents were more likely to have federal governmental experience than their Democratic colleagues in the years prior to World War II. Relatedly, judges appointed by Democratic presidents were more likely to have state-level governmental experience during

TABLE 2.4. U.S. Courts of Appeals Judges' Experience in Government and Politics, by Presidential Party and Time Period (in percentages)

Attribute	Period 1 (1925–36) Dem. Pres. (n = 30)	Period 1 (1925–36) Rep. Pres. (n = 49)	Period 2 (1937–45) Dem. Pres. (n = 48)	Period 2 (1937–45) Rep. Pres. (n = 14)	Period 3 (1946–60) Dem. Pres. (n = 46)	Period 3 (1946–60) Rep. Pres. (n = 57)	Period 4 (1961–69) Dem. Pres. (n = 84)	Period 4 (1961–69) Rep. Pres. (n = 27)	Period 5 (1970–88) Dem. Pres. (n = 114)	Period 5 (1970–88) Rep. Pres. (n = 157)
Governmental experience (any type)	86.7	91.8	79.2	92.9	89.1	85.9	85.7	85.2	78.9	79.0
Federal government	76.7	89.8	75.0	100	78.3	78.9	58.6	77.8	73.7	76.4
State/local government	66.7	57.1	60.4	42.9	60.9	56.1	45.1	44.4	57.0	45.9
Political experience										
U.S. Congress	13.3	8.2	10.4	0	8.7	3.5	4.8	7.4	3.5	3.2
State/local legislature/government	20.0	22.5	16.7	7.1	15.2	19.3	19.1	11.1	18.4	9.6

this time period. Over time, these partisan differences declined, but did not disappear altogether. Appointment cohorts did not differ in one respect: those selected by presidents of both parties were not likely to have previous experience as a member of Congress.

Legal Careers

The varying selection procedures adopted by appointing presidents appear to affect the nature and extent of their nominees' previous judicial experiences. Similar to the findings regarding career paths in table 2.3, the data in table 2.5 indicate that judges sitting on the bench in the early years (1925–36) who were appointed by Republican presidents tended to have previous judicial experience. In contrast, early appointees of Democratic presidents were more likely to have judicial experience in state court, relative to their Republican counterparts. These partisan differences declined somewhat over time, particularly after 1960. Since 1960, approximately 55 to 60 percent of those appointed to the appeals courts have had previous judicial experience.

Prior to their appointment, judges' careers in the legal profession have varied by party of the appointing president and over time. For example, appointees of Republican presidents in the early years of the courts tended to have state-level prosecutorial experience, when compared to their colleagues appointed by Democratic presidents. Most judges across appointing administrations tended to have experience in private practice. In the most recent period, a higher percentage of appointees had previous experience as a law professor.

Personal Attributes

The demographic profile of judges on the U.S. Courts of Appeals suggests very little variation in their social backgrounds, particularly in the years prior to 1970 (see table 2.6). Most judges have been Caucasian male Protestants in their mid-fifties at the time of appointment. To the extent that differences in religious backgrounds exist, it appears that Democratic presidents, perhaps as a result of their constituencies, were more likely to appoint Catholic judges in the period prior to 1970. Since the 1970s, President Carter's judicial selection strategy and changes in the legal profession itself have contributed to diversity on the U.S. Courts of Appeals with

TABLE 2.5. U.S. Courts of Appeals Judges' Legal and Judicial Backgrounds, by Presidential Party and Time Period (in percentages)

Attribute	Period 1 (1925–36) Dem. Pres. (n = 30)	Period 1 (1925–36) Rep. Pres. (n = 49)	Period 2 (1937–45) Dem. Pres. (n = 48)	Period 2 (1937–45) Rep. Pres. (n = 14)	Period 3 (1946–60) Dem. Pres. (n = 46)	Period 3 (1946–60) Rep. Pres. (n = 57)	Period 4 (1961–69) Dem. Pres. (n = 84)	Period 4 (1961–69) Rep. Pres. (n = 27)	Period 5 (1970–88) Dem. Pres. (n = 114)	Period 5 (1970–88) Rep. Pres. (n = 157)
Judicial experience	60.0	83.7	52.1	85.7	54.4	68.4	58.3	55.6	56.1	58.0
Promoted from district court	23.3	63.3	29.2	50.0	30.4	42.1	39.3	40.7	34.2	44.6
Any previous experience in district court	30.0	65.3	31.3	50.0	39.1	43.9	39.3	44.4	36.0	44.6
Other federal court	0	4.1	0	7.1	0	3.5	0	7.4	0.9	1.3
State supreme court	33.3	14.3	16.7	21.4	13.0	10.5	8.3	0.0	8.8	9.6
State/local lower court	30.0	30.6	16.7	21.4	17.4	33.3	28.6	22.2	26.3	19.8
Attorney experience										
Prosecutor (state court)	16.7	34.7	16.7	28.6	26.1	29.8	25.0	22.2	24.6	23.6
U.S. Attorney (or Asst. U.S. Attorney)	20.0	18.4	6.3	28.6	17.4	15.8	13.1	18.5	15.8	14.0
Law professor	13.3	14.3	27.1	21.4	19.6	12.3	21.4	11.1	26.3	24.2
Private practice	87.8	90.0	87.5	71.4	91.3	100	94.0	100	93.9	94.9

TABLE 2.6. U.S. Courts of Appeals Judges' Demographic Characteristics, by Presidential Party and Time Period (in percentages)

Attribute	Period 1 (1925–36) Dem. Pres. (n = 30)	Period 1 (1925–36) Rep. Pres. (n = 49)	Period 2 (1937–45) Dem. Pres. (n = 48)	Period 2 (1937–45) Rep. Pres. (n = 14)	Period 3 (1946–60) Dem. Pres. (n = 46)	Period 3 (1946–60) Rep. Pres. (n = 57)	Period 4 (1961–69) Dem. Pres. (n = 84)	Period 4 (1961–69) Rep. Pres. (n = 27)	Period 5 (1970–88) Dem. Pres. (n = 114)	Period 5 (1970–88) Rep. Pres. (n = 157)
Median age at time of appointment	57	56	52	54	56	56	53	61	53	53
Religion										
Protestant	83.4	93.9	83.3	92.9	71.8	82.5	66.7	77.8	59.6	64.9
Catholic	13.3	2.0	14.6	0	21.7	10.5	8.3	0	22.0	23.2
Jewish	3.3	4.1	2.1	7.1	6.5	7.0	25.0	22.2	16.5	11.9
Race										
Caucasian	100	100	100	100	95.6	100	96.4	100	87.7	98.8
African-American					2.2		3.6		10.5	0.6
Hispanic					2.2				1.8	0.6
Gender (percent male)	96.7	100	100	100	97.8	100	98.8	100	89.5	97.4
Education										
Public law school	23.3	28.6	31.3	22.9	28.3	43.9	34.5	44.4	38.2	61.8
Public undergraduate	26.7	20.4	7.1	14.3	26.1	36.8	29.8	33.3	41.1	58.9

increasing numbers of minorities and women occupying seats on the circuit courts.

Staffing by Circuit

The portrait above suggests substantial variation in the characteristics of judges on the U.S. Courts of Appeals over time and by party of the appointing president. Underlying this variation, however, may be differences at the circuit level. Our earlier examination of the partisan balance on the U.S. Courts of Appeals found judges appointed by Republicans made up a substantial majority of the bench in the first (1925–36), third (1946–60), and fifth (1970–88) periods. However, circuit-level variation in the partisan makeup of the bench is evident in table 2.7.

From 1925 through 1936, judges appointed by Democrats slightly outnumbered those appointed by Republicans in the First, Fifth, and Seventh Circuits. In contrast, judges appointed by Republican presidents dominated the bench in the Fourth, Sixth, Eighth, and DC circuits. Aggregate data on the post–World War II period (1946–60) characterized the bench as being one where Republican appointees were in the majority. Yet judges appointed by Democratic presidents were in the majority in the First, Third, Fifth, Seventh, and DC Circuits. In those circuits where Republican appointees were in the majority, they clearly dominated in sheer numbers (the Second, Fourth, Sixth, and Eighth Circuits). Aggregate data for the most recent period (1970–88) depict a bench where appointees of Republican presidents managed to hold a majority on the appeals courts. However, again, the nature and extent of this majority varied by circuit. In the Second, Third, Seventh, and Eighth Circuits, judges appointed by Republicans substantially outnumbered their Democratic colleagues. Interestingly, in the Fifth and Eleventh Circuits, the number of sitting judges appointed by Democratic presidents actually exceeded the number of judges appointed by Republicans. In the DC Circuit, and to a lesser extent the Ninth Circuit, the judges were almost equally divided.

The number of judges with experience as a federal trial court judge also varied by circuit. The frequencies for the most recent period were particularly striking. More judges in the northeastern and southern circuits had previous experience as a federal district court judge than in other circuits. The highly visible, often politicized appointments to the DC Circuit tended to result in the selection of judges who were less likely to have previous experience in federal district court across all time periods.

TABLE 2.7. U.S. Courts of Appeals Judges: An Intercircuit Profile

Period 1 (1925–36)

	1st (n = 5)	2nd (n = 8)	3rd (n = 4)	4th (n = 6)	5th (n = 7)	6th (n = 8)	7th (n = 7)	8th (n = 12)	9th (n = 13)	10th (n = 3)	DC (n = 6)
Number appointed by Democrats	3	3	2	1	4	2	4	4	5	1	1
Number appointed by Republicans	2	5	2	5	3	6	3	8	8	2	5
Number of judges with previous experience in federal district court	1	4	3	3	4	6	2	7	6	2	3

Period 2 (1937–45)

	1st (n = 6)	2nd (n = 4)	3rd (n = 12)	4th (n = 2)	5th (n = 4)	6th (n = 6)	7th (n = 4)	8th (n = 2)	9th (n = 6)	10th (n = 4)	DC (n = 12)
Number appointed by Democrats	4	4	10	1	3	5	3	2	5	3	8
Number appointed by Republicans	2	0	2	1	1	1	1	0	1	1	4
Number of judges with previous experience in federal district court	2	2	5	1	2	4	1	0	1	3	1

Period 3 (1946–60)

	1st (n = 4)	2nd (n = 12)	3rd (n = 6)	4th (n = 6)	5th (n = 14)	6th (n = 7)	7th (n = 13)	8th (n = 11)	9th (n = 16)	10th (n = 5)	DC (n = 9)
Number appointed by Democrats	3	2	5	1	8	1	7	4	7	2	6
Number appointed by Republicans	1	10	1	5	6	6	6	7	9	3	3
Number of judges with previous experience in federal district court	3	5	4	3	6	5	4	4	4	2	3

Period 4   (1961–69)

	1st (n = 4)	2nd (n = 6)	3rd (n = 14)	4th (n = 5)	5th (n = 19)	6th (n = 12)	7th (n = 9)	8th (n = 9)	9th (n = 12)	10th (n = 6)	DC (n = 15)
Number appointed by Democrats	4	6	11	5	12	9	6	8	7	6	10
Number appointed by Republicans	0	0	3	0	7	3	3	1	5	0	5
Number of judges with previous experience in federal district court	1	3	5	4	9	7	2	4	5	1	4

Period 5   (1970–88)

	1st (n = 8)	2nd (n = 25)	3rd (n = 22)	4th (n = 19)	5th (n = 43)	6th (n = 27)	7th (n = 21)	8th (n = 20)	9th (n = 44)	10th (n = 19)	11th (n = 15)	DC (n = 21)
Number appointed by Democrats	4	6	8	8	25	12	6	7	20	8	8	10
Number appointed by Republicans	4	19	14	11	18	15	15	13	24	11	7	11
Number of judges with previous experience in federal district court	5	13	11	11	18	16	7	8	11	6	7	4

Note: Eight judges appointed by Democrats and five judges appointed by Republicans left the Fifth Circuit to sit on the Eleventh Circuit in 1982.

Conclusion

The impact of judicial appointments is felt long after the president's tenure in office expires. Democratic presidents Roosevelt and Carter, in particular, appeared to disproportionately affect the makeup of the lower courts due to well-timed judges bills creating new seats. As a result, the influx of their appointees tended to minimize the effects of judicial selection during the two-term presidencies of their Republican successors, Eisenhower and Reagan. Overall, however, judges sitting on the bench in each period reflected on the party of appointing presidents. As a result, one would expect judicial policy in these courts to be more likely to reflect the preferences of Republican presidents in the first (1925–36), third (1946–60), and fifth (1970–88) periods. Judicial decision making in the second (1937–45) and fourth (1961–69) periods should parallel the views of Democratic presidents.

These data also indicate that over time, presidents selected men and women with differing experiences and career paths. Those differences associated with the party of the appointing president were more pronounced prior to 1960. In the early years of the courts of appeals, judges appointed by Republican presidents tended to have previous federal judicial experience. In contrast, those appointed by Democrats were more likely to have had career paths that indicated strong ties to the home state. Over time, these partisan differences declined so that judges sitting on the bench after 1960 tended to be similar to one another in their career experiences. Differences by appointing president remained, however, when comparing the demographic attributes of those selected. In particular, the efforts of President Carter to recruit qualified minorities and women resulted in a bench that was more diversified. Overall, these data also indicate changes in the kinds of judges sitting on the bench that may be attributed to growth and specialization within the legal profession. Unlike judges in the early years, those appointed since 1970 have had more varied initial experiences, including appointments to law faculty and clerkships in federal court.

The partisan makeup of the bench also varied by circuit. For example, judges appointed by Republican presidents never dominated the First, Fifth, or Eleventh Circuits throughout the periods examined. Since 1970, intercircuit differences in the partisan makeup of the courts were quite apparent. In the Second and Seventh Circuits, judges sitting on the bench who were appointed by Republican presidents outnumbered those appointed by Democrats by a nearly three-to-one margin; while in other circuits, such as the First, Ninth, and DC Circuits, there were roughly equal numbers of Democratic and Republican appointees sitting on the bench during this time period. Partisan imbalances would suggest the potential for circuit-level differences in decision making that reflect on the policy preferences of the majority. Ultimately, variation in circuit precedent may contribute to the potential for forum shopping by litigants seeking a favorable outcome. Partisan differences by circuit also may reduce cohesion within the circuit. For example, in some courts (such as the DC and Ninth Circuits) where Democratic and Republican appointees were roughly equal in numbers, one would expect higher dissent rates.

From a longitudinal perspective, many similarities and differences in the attributes of judges were suggested by these analyses. Judges still tend to be Caucasian, male, and Protestant; yet more diversity exists on the bench today. Over time, the number of appeals court judges promoted from district court positions had not fluctuated widely; yet their paths to the bench now include more varied initial experiences. In the remaining chapters, we turn to exploring the consequences of continuity and change in the staffing of the bench over time as well as other factors that influence the policy-making role of the U.S. Courts of Appeals.

CHAPTER 3

Setting the Agenda: Judicial Business in the U.S. Courts of Appeals

Introduction

As the first and final appellate court for most litigants in the federal legal system, the U.S. Courts of Appeals perform an important function in dispute resolution and norm enforcement. These courts' work centers on detecting legal error in trial court or agency decisions. In most cases, the circuit courts affirm the judgment below. Still, substantial variety and diversity underlie this high volume of "ordinary appeals." In a snapshot view of a "day in the life of a judge" on the U.S. Courts of Appeals, Judge Coffin (1994) describes the typical cases scheduled for oral argument: a claim brought by a student under the Rehabilitation Act, an appeal from a criminal conviction for cocaine possession where the defendant alleges error in jury instructions, an indemnity case involving the insurance of businesses being held liable for cleanup of toxic waste, an employment discrimination claim, a labor-management case being appealed from the National Labor Relations Board, and an appeal concerning a habeas corpus petition filed by a state prisoner. The high volume of diverse cases is manageable as a result of their ability to screen and therefore consolidate cases so that the "treatment" received by litigants in these courts varies. As a result, characterizing judicial business at the circuit level is multifaceted. Ultimately, scholars are interested in learning about any patterns in case types before the courts; however, works that focus on studying cases commenced give a sense of the kinds of cases being appealed but they do not provide an accurate picture of the kinds of policy-making issues addressed by these courts. Due to the large number of cases that are procedurally terminated,[1] analyses of all cases disposed of by the U.S. Courts of Appeals similarly do not provide a portrait of judicial business. As a result, we focus here on examining the kinds of issues raised in published decisions as these cases will provide a sense of the policy-making concerns that make up the judicial work load.

Diversity may characterize the activity of these appellate courts, but social scientists early on noted that the varying legal issues and types of cases in the U.S. Courts of Appeals were not random. Research focused on unraveling these patterns has contributed to our understanding of these courts since the policy impact of their decisions depends on the kinds of appeals before them. The U.S. Courts of Appeals do not enjoy a discretionary docket; therefore, the kinds of cases heard in these courts will reflect, on one level, the kinds of disputes addressed by the federal legal system. However, all cases are not appealed, and most cases in recent years have not been accompanied by a published decision. In this chapter, we examine how the business of the courts of appeals has evolved over time and the factors that shaped, and continue to shape, the issue agendas of these courts. To guide our inquiry, previous scholarship suggests several influences that may be expected to affect the types of cases that are litigated and appealed in the federal court system. Although much of this prior research focuses on the propensity to litigate generally, these findings are relevant to understanding the kinds of disputes before appellate courts as well. For example, influences that have been found to shape the initial decision to litigate, such as the socioeconomic environment and the political context, may be expected to affect the kinds of cases heard before any court, regardless of its level. In addition, the composition of cases before the U.S. Courts of Appeals will be a reflection of litigants' decisions to appeal. For example, litigants who lost in the trial court may be more likely to pursue an appeal when trends in Supreme Court decision making would indicate High Court support for the position taken by that losing litigant. Institutional norms and practices also may affect both the decision to pursue litigation in a particular circuit or appeal to the circuit court. In this respect, the concentration of issue types at the circuit level may be related to forum-shopping where litigation strategies take into account the appellate court's receptivity to their claim. For example, Howard (1981) found the circuit court of appeals with the smallest share of patent cases (compared to other circuits) was perceived to be unreceptive to patents. Other studies note that decision-making rules and norms in the U.S. Courts of Appeals also are developed at the circuit level (Barrow and Walker 1988; Van Winkle 1996). Finally, each of these influences—the socioeconomic environment, the political context, the legal environment, and institutional practices—will affect not only decisions to litigate and appeal, but also the attention given by circuit court judges to particular issues. For example, newly passed legislative enactments and ambiguously worded Supreme Court precedent will require circuit court judges to devote more time and thought to the issues. The need to establish precedent, at the circuit level, in these gray areas also may increase the likelihood of publishing the court decision.

Social Development Theory and the Business of Appellate Courts

At the most basic level, characteristics of society affect the level and kinds of disputes taken to court. For judicial scholars analyzing caseloads, these characteristics are relevant because courts can only address those demands that are brought by litigants. Caseloads change in conjunction with changes in conditions surrounding litigants so that as populations have grown and society becomes more complex, more disputes arise and result in increased litigation (Sarat and Grossman 1975; Baum, Goldman, and Sarat 1981). This perspective views the role of law and courts in society as one that reacts to the transformation of social and economic circumstances. Proponents of social development theory also argue that courts are particularly important when there are "thrusts" in development that destroy existing relationship structures requiring the litigation of disputes to restore order (McIntosh 1983). During these times of transition, the function of the courts is critical to the resolution of private disputes, but these same changes in the existing social order should lead legislatures and administrative agencies to act as well. Therefore, the business of the courts is initially affected by changes in private dispute resolution; then, later, caseloads will change as the courts address litigation associated with the passage of legislation that also deals with the same changes in the social order.

Over time, the development of society should not only affect litigation rates, but also the subject matter of litigation. In their analysis of litigation in the Second, Fifth, and Ninth Circuit Courts of Appeals, Baum, Goldman, and Sarat (1981) found that the kinds of private economic cases before the courts shifted over the course of the twentieth century and that some of these trends were attributed to social change. For example, they attribute the decline in real property disputes in the Fifth and Ninth Circuit to be associated with the evolution of disputes over land ownership questions during the time period. As land became more settled in the west and southwest, real property disputes declined. In contrast, they found very few real property disputes in the urbanized states of the Second Circuit throughout the time period. This theoretical perspective also was supported by their overall findings that from 1895 to 1975 public law disputes gradually replaced private economic disputes.

The development of society also may contribute to the rise in criminal cases on the federal courts' docket. Increased involvement by the federal government to address problems associated with the rise of violent crime in the twentieth century has contributed to a tremendous rise in criminal cases in the federal courts. In particular, legal commentators note the alarming rise in the number of federal drug prosecutions as part of the governmental effort to combat problems created by drug use and abuse (Posner 1996). Not surprisingly, empirical studies document growth in criminal appeals over the 1960s and 1970s (Howard 1981; Davis and Songer 1989). Social development also may affect the type of offense raised in criminal appeals. Baum, Goldman, and Sarat (1981) found the criminal offenses raised in cases before the U.S. Courts of Appeals had changed, with crimes against persons and property becoming more commonplace over time.

Social development theory appears to be helpful in explaining changes in the types of issues being litigated over time, but it also may account for other, geographically based variation. In this respect, judicial business may be expected to reflect the regional character of the area of the country defined by circuit boundaries. For example, in one analysis, a comparison of the business of three circuits led one scholar to conclude that the Second Circuit had a higher proportion of "staple" private economic appeals as a result of the regional commercial centers in the Northeast (Howard 1981). Yet other, more recent studies find little support for regional variation in judicial business. Davis and Songer (1989) found circuit-level differences in the kinds of cases heard across the twelve circuits in 1984, but these differences were not regional in character. Harrington and Ward (1995) similarly found no support for this theoretical perspective: their results indicate that circuits with more private civil appeals had lower levels of per capita income.

Political Context and the Issue Agenda

The posture taken by the other branches of government can shape the agenda of the federal courts in one of several ways. For many interest groups and individuals, litigation is an alternate form of political activity. If the other branches are not addressing or resolving problems experienced by a particular interest, this "out group" may turn to the courts to address their issue (McIntosh 1990). Early studies of group-sponsored litigation support the notion that those who are politically disadvantaged in majoritarian arenas, such as legislatures, turn to the courts to advance their policy interest (Cortner 1968). More recent analyses suggest that interest groups increasingly turn to the judiciary to counter the presence of opposing interests (Epstein 1985). From this perspective, the agenda of the lower courts will be affected as litigants pursue issues unaddressed by the legislative and executive branches in the judicial system. Other interests similarly may pursue litigation to protect those political gains achieved in the other branches of government and counter an opposing interest. Unlike the legislative and executive branches, the courts provide more policy-making opportunities for "disadvantaged" litigants as a result of a legal system that is geared toward protecting individual interests and satisfying due process of law.

The executive and legislative branches also may alter the agenda of the lower courts through their own lawmaking. The passage of statutes will contribute to litigation as even clearly phrased statutory language may be interpreted differently. In particular, the period immediately following the passage of the statute requires the courts to figure out the meaning of particular statutory provisions, how to apply statutes to situations that were unanticipated by the legislature, and how to resolve conflicts between statutes and other sources of law. For example, following the passage of the National Environmental Policy Act in 1969, claims litigated in federal court during the 1970s required circuit court judges to deal with important questions unaddressed by Congress: what constitutes a "major federal action" that requires an Environmental Impact Statement, who should write it, when it should be written, and what kinds of actions are exempt (Wenner 1989).

"Lawmaking" by administrative agencies charged with implementation of statutory policy also may lead to litigation where rules are challenged by varying interests. For some agencies, the increased utilization of rule making has shifted dispute resolution to the U.S. Courts of Appeals where most agency decisions are appealed. Policy decisions of the executive branch also can fuel litigation in the federal courts. For example, officials in the Social Security Administration occasionally alter eligibility criteria for disability benefits, leading many claimants to pursue litigation. The executive branch also can initiate litigation as it did in the 1970s when officials pursued in federal court the overpayment of veterans' benefits to individuals or sought judicial enforcement of desegregation laws against several school systems. Executive branch decisions regarding the enforcement of federal criminal statutes aimed at a variety of offenses, including organized crime and drug-related behavior, also affect the federal courts' docket.

Legal Environment

As intermediate appellate courts, the U.S. Courts of Appeals decide cases that are subject to review by the Supreme Court. Consequently, the nature and direction of decisions of the upper court may affect the disputes brought to the lower courts. For example, the due process "revolution" of the Warren Court likely fueled claims raised by criminal defendants assisted by the availability of legal counsel and court rules giving petitions filed in forma pauperis more favorable treatment. Therefore, changes in the composition of the upper court may serve as cues to litigants in the lower courts to test existing doctrine. The nature of the upper court precedent also will affect the issue agenda of lower courts. If the Supreme Court creates a new area of legal doctrine through its decisions, or appears divided in an approach to a particular issue, more appeals are likely to be heard in that area because existing case law is unclear.

Being the first appellate forum affects judicial business in the circuit courts as well. The implied right of one appeal leads to a high volume of routine cases with litigants who have nothing to lose. For example, criminal defendants looking at prison time may appeal even if they are not likely to win. Similarly, plaintiffs in civil cases where attorney fee-shifting takes place may be more likely to appeal. The types of issues raised in the initial appeal necessarily differ from those in the trial court or administrative tribunal. Whereas the trial court focuses on fact-finding and norm enforcement (Carp and Rowland 1983), the appellate court turns to examining questions surrounding legal error in the proceeding below. As a result, procedural issues are more likely to be raised in the circuit courts. In courts and years where judges are pressured with high caseloads, procedural questions may provide the framework for the decision-making process as they are less costly in terms of time and resources.

Finally, the role of the U.S. Courts of Appeals will be influenced by changes in its jurisdiction. Changes initiated by Congress or by the Judicial Conference[2] have the potential to dramatically limit or expand the types of appeals in the circuit courts. For example, changes in the 1970s virtually removed criminal cases from the jurisdiction of the U.S. Courts of Appeals for the DC Circuit. Over time, Congress has altered judicial review of some administrative agency decisions and increased the threshold dollar amount for diversity of citizenship cases. More recently, changes have been initiated to limit federal court review of habeas corpus petitions. The creation of legislative courts and other specialized courts also may limit the jurisdiction of Article 3 courts to hear some kinds of disputes, such as those that deal with patents or copyright protection.

Institutional Practices

To minimize costs in litigation, including appeals, litigants and their counsel are likely to gauge the "receptivity" of the circuit court to their claim. As suggested by Howard (1981), for some litigants and issues, this litigation strategy will shape the decision where to litigate as well as whether to appeal. The result may be a concentration of some types of cases in particular circuits. Empirical research does suggest circuit-level differences in case types that are not related to region or the socioeconomic characteristics of the population (Songer and Davis 1989; Harrington and Ward 1995). The reasons for these differences may stem from specific institutional practices that influence the decision to appeal (Harrington and Ward 1995). For example, circuits vary in their practices that govern which cases are granted oral argument (Oakley 1991). In the 1980s, the U.S. Court of Appeals for the Eighth Circuit decided to grant oral argument to cases involving social security disability determinations; however, many other circuit courts routinely assign these cases to staff attorneys who review the record and make a recommendation regarding disposition (Haire and Lindquist 1997). Not surprisingly, the publication rate for social security disability appeals is dramatically higher in the Eighth Circuit. With more precedent available to them, litigants' attorneys in the Eighth Circuit would be more likely to pursue an appeal regarding social security disability claims in this court as it appears to be more focused on developing the legal issues raised in these cases. Relatedly, litigants in circuits with high reversal rates in certain substantive areas would be more likely to pursue an appeal. On the other hand, if appeals court judges routinely affirm trial court decisions in a substantive area, litigants would be discouraged from pursuing litigation at the appellate level. As we suggested in the second chapter, the receptivity of the circuit to litigants and issues may vary as a result of the ideological mix of judges sitting on that court's bench.

Each of the perspectives outlined above suggests that the agendas of the U.S. Courts of Appeals will vary over time and by circuit as a result of shifts in society, action (or inaction) of the other branches of government, legal influences associated with the judicial hierarchy, and decision-making practices and norms of selected circuits. In the analyses that follow, we profile the issues raised in decisions of the U.S. Courts of Appeals and assess whether these perspectives account for the types of decisions issued by these courts.

Judicial Business: The Big Picture

An initial assessment of the broad issue areas addressed by the U.S. Courts of Appeals is provided in table 3.1. The categories reflect the percentage of the total decisions issued during the time period that fell within that category. If a case raised two issues, each of which fell into a different category, they were counted for both categories. For example, if the case raised a civil rights claim and a criminal issue, it was counted in both "civil rights" and "criminal." To examine more closely trends within these time periods, figure 3.1 plots the percentage of judicial business devoted to each of these categories by year.

The data presented in table 3.1 and figure 3.1 indicate substantial shifts in judicial business over time. Appeals in the early years (1925–36) frequently raised economic issues in litigation between private parties. In a typical case before the Sixth Circuit, a salesman appealed the decision of the district court denying him payment for commissions associated with the sale of a machine that polished automobile crankshafts. Finding no breach of contract, the court held for the defendant, *Strong v. Scharner* 67 F.2d 687 (6th Cir. 1933). Over time, judicial attention to disputes between private parties has declined, but such disputes still make up nearly a fourth of the cases decided with published opinion. While continuity character-

TABLE 3.1.   Judicial Business in the U.S. Courts of Appeals (by time period, in percentages)

Issue Area	1925–36	1937–45	1946–60	1961–69	1970–88
Criminal	11.8	13.3	21.1	32.3	32.3
Civil liberties	0.5	0.8	2.6	1.9	5.0
Civil rights	1.2	0.9	1.9	3.9	13.5
Public economic	31.4	37.9	31.3	24.3	25.0
Private economic	48.5	43.6	38.4	35.2	24.5

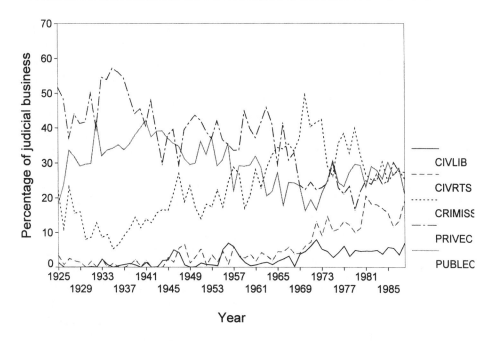

FIG. 3.1. Decisions of the U.S. Courts of Appeals, by policy area

izes some legal issues, the questions presented in more recent cases reflect on the increasing complexity of commercial relationships and high-stakes disputes. For example, in *Apex Oil Co. v. Vanguard Oil and Service Co.*, 760 F.2d 417 (2d Cir. 1985), the court upheld the district court's determination that a breach of contract had occurred with an award to the corporate plaintiff of over $1,000,000. In contrast to the one-page decision issued fifty years earlier, this seven-page decision dealt with intricacies surrounding the interpretation of New York state law as it considered whether a business transaction via telex was an enforceable contract. In these "routine" appeals separated by a fifty-year period, similar principles of contract law emerged, but technological changes and an increase in the stakes involved altered the legal questions in the more recent case. Similar developments have contributed to the rise of other private litigation over economic issues, including products liability claims, where principles of tort law have evolved to reflect on changes in society, including shifts in attitudes regarding the responsibilities of the business sector.

Although there has been a substantial decline in attention given to private law issues, the percentage of judicial work load devoted to analyzing public law economic questions has remained relatively stable. Analyses of cases commenced in the U.S. Courts of Appeals indicate that economic disputes have continued to rise over time (Harrington and Ward 1995; Posner 1996). Yet, the picture here suggests that published decisions are now less concentrated in this area.

In contrast to economic decisions, judicial attention to criminal cases rises over time. This rise may be due in part to changes in the decision-making calculus regarding appeals. Posner (1996) found the appeal rate of federal criminal cases in 1960 to be 25.1 percent, but by 1983 the figure had climbed to 94.5 percent. He attributed this change to the passage of the Criminal Justice Act of 1964 that funds the appointment of counsel in the courts of appeals, thereby making it possible for every federal criminal defendant to appeal his or her conviction. The rise in criminal cases also may reflect other changes in the legal environment associated with decisional trends in the Supreme Court. Most legal scholars agree that the Warren Court was more receptive to claims of the criminally accused. The series of High Court decisions associated with the "due process revolution," including the extension of the exclusionary rule to state court proceedings, likely fueled claims of state prisoners in the federal courts. In addition, the reinterpretation of the Habeas Corpus Act of 1867 extended federal habeas corpus to persons in state custody. On the other hand, decisions of the more conservative Burger and Rehnquist Courts that have clarified and limited Warren Court precedent may have contributed to the flattening-out of this trend in the last period.

The passage of time also corresponds to the rise of civil rights issues before the U.S. Courts of Appeals. The decisions of the Warren Court helped to fuel litigation associated with the Equal Protection Clause of the Fourteenth Amendment, contributing to the involvement of lower federal courts in the implementation of desegregation decisions. However, more important, Congress passed a series of statutes in the 1960s that established federally protected civil rights. The passage of these civil rights acts and judicial reinterpretations of the Reconstruction civil rights statutes[3] created damage remedies for violations of federal rights by state officers. Many areas of these civil rights statutory law have still been relatively unsettled in the 1970s and 1980s as a result of shifts in Supreme Court decisions dealing with employment discrimination and legislative amendments to existing statutes protecting the rights of pregnant women, the disabled, the elderly, and other groups in the workplace. Overall, changes in the receptivity of these courts to claims of discrimination also may be due to changes in support for these claims in society (Rosenberg 1991).

Similar to civil rights issues, circuit court decisions involving civil liberties also have risen over time. The findings reported in table 3.1 for these issue areas parallel the well-known shift in the Supreme Court's agenda from one dominated by economic concerns to one dominated by civil rights and liberties claims. The estimates reported in table 3.2 more clearly illustrate the dramatic increase over time in the raw numbers of civil rights and liberties decisions of the circuit courts. Still, given the high number of appeals raising economic issues, these issue areas occupy a "minority" position in the overall assessment of judicial business on the appeals courts.

Economic Issues: Private and Public Law Disputes

The broad profile presented above is helpful in sorting out general trends; however, to examine more carefully changes in issue agendas, we profile case categories within each of these broadly defined areas and begin this stage of our analysis by focusing on economic issues. The results presented in table 3.1 suggested the attention given to private law economic issues had fallen over time, but economic issues involving the government as a party remained relatively stable. Table 3.3 provides further evidence that in early years judges heard and submitted for publication decisions in many areas of staple litigation: patent/copyright, contracts, tax, debt collection, and bankruptcy. However, with the exception of contracts, over time, the attention devoted to some of these staples fell. Why?

One potential reason for this shift focuses on the legal environment and institutional practices of the circuit courts. Over time, caseloads have

TABLE 3.2. Judicial Business in the U.S. Courts of Appeals: Number of Published Decisions by Issue Area (estimated annual average, by time period)

Issue Area	1925–36	1937–45	1946–60	1961–69	1970–88
Criminal	258	301	491	1,164	1,729
Civil liberties	11	18	60	68	268
Civil rights	26	20	44	141	723
Public economic	687	858	728	876	1,338
Private economic	1,061	987	1,126	1,269	1,312

clearly increased in the U.S. Courts of Appeals, even though scholars debate the magnitude and consequences of this increase (Posner 1996). As a result of rising caseloads, judges spend less time on "ordinary" appeals. Of those that do require judicial attention, most usually do not result in a published decision and therefore are no longer a dominant part of the judge's work load. In some instances, specialized federal trial courts were created by Congress, such as the Tax Court, Claims Court, and Court of International Trade, to meet the caseloads and unique legal issues associated with that case type. In addition, the use of magistrates in district courts and bankruptcy judges has relegated some cases to a different track at the trial level. Similar dynamics have been at work at the appellate level. The Court of Claims and the U.S. Court of Customs and Patent Appeals was turned into a constitutional court in 1982: the Court of Appeals for the Federal Circuit. This change altered the jurisdiction of the other courts of appeals and reduced the kinds and number of appeals relating to trademarks, patents, foreign trade, and some claims against the federal government (Baum 1991). Today, in several circuits, appeals may be screened by staff attorneys who assist in the identification of issues, identify cases that require oral argument, and propose dispositions for some "ordinary" appeals. As a result, certain kinds of routine cases have been effectively removed (or at least reduced) from the appeals courts' issue agenda.

Other possible reasons for shifts in the issues over time concern social development and the political context. The state of the economy will affect many issues in the federal courts. Debt collection cases were more likely in

TABLE 3.3.   Economic Issues in the U.S. Courts of Appeals (as a percentage of economics decisions, by time period)

Issue Area	1925–36	1937–45	1946–60	1961–69	1970–88
Admiralty	4.2	2.3	2.6	2.8	2.0
Antitrust/mergers	0.3	0.7	1.5	2.8	3.0
Bankruptcy	7.2	14.9	6.0	5.5	5.7
Contracts	9.4	7.0	9.9	9.4	9.3
Debt collection	6.8	3.2	1.7	1.8	2.4
Economic regulation	5.4	6.1	9.2	6.8	13.3
Individual benefits	3.9	2.5	1.5	2.8	6.2
Labor	1.0	6.0	10.7	18.3	16.4
Patent/trademark copyright	12.4	10.0	6.2	5.7	3.3
Private property	1.5	1.0	0.3	0.2	0.1
Tax	16.6	24.2	17.6	13.2	7.8
Torts	0.5	1.4	3.1	1.8	1.5

the first period, an era marked by the Depression. However, these cases were less likely during the post–World War II economic boom. As corporations increasingly acquired other corporations, judicial attention to antitrust and merger issues emerged. The political context also may account for some shifts in the issue agenda. The growth of the welfare state (created by statutes) over time corresponds to the rise in attention given to cases associated with claims for benefits. In particular, during the 1970s and 1980s, administrations faced with the burgeoning costs of welfare began to restrict claims, leaving individuals to turn to the courts for remedies. A number of studies note the explosion of case filings in federal district courts associated with SSI disability claims in the early 1980s (Mezey 1988). Ultimately, these decisions affect the courts of appeals' work load as the circuits had to establish precedent regarding the rights of welfare recipients.[4]

The creation of new regulatory areas in the 1970s also contributed to the changing caseload profile. The passage of statutes designed to protect consumers, the environment, regulation of transportation, and utilities all contributed to increased judicial attention to issues of economic regulation in the U.S. Courts of Appeals. The rise of labor unions and the passage of statutes governing labor relations also contributed to litigation and review of administrative agency decisions in this issue area. Beginning in the 1960s, decisions examining labor issues have become a staple of judicial business. Trends in these decisions, most of which are petitions emanating from orders by the National Labor Relations Board (NLRB), reflect on several dynamics that are not easily explained. To begin with, since 1960, the absolute number of unionized workers has increased, but the percentage of the labor force that is unionized has declined. Complaints to the NLRB alleging unfair labor practices increased dramatically during this time frame, which some scholars argue was due to employers engaging in tactics that were more likely to be in violation of the National Labor Relations Act as part of an overall effort to keep labor costs down (Weiler 1983). In addition to contests between labor and management, litigation has evolved over time, as many appeals now involve disputes between rival unions, unions and their membership, and union members and leaders.

Criminal Issues: A Closer Look at Offense Types and Habeas Corpus Petitions

The data presented in table 3.4 suggest that, of the relatively few criminal decisions making up the judicial work load in the early period, most cases involved nonviolent offenses, particularly actions related to violations during Prohibition.[5] Over time, their work load increasingly involved cases where violent crimes had been committed. The federal "war on drugs" waged by both the legislative and executive branches has led to an increase in statutes dealing with drug offenses as well as federal prosecutions (and appeals) in cases involving drug offenses. With the exception of the first period (which includes Prohibition), the percentage of criminal decisions dealing with drug offenses has risen substantially over time.

Changes in legal doctrine during the Warren Court likely contributed to the jump in state habeas corpus decisions brought by prisoners in 1961 through 1969. Again, as noted earlier, it is equally likely that the composition of both the Supreme Court and the lower courts, increasingly dominated by appointees of Republican presidents, contributed to the flattening out of this trend in the latest period.

Civil Rights Issues in the 1970s and 1980s

Civil rights issues did not occupy a prominent place on the courts of appeals' dockets until the 1970s. As a result, our profile of this issue area focuses on case types that make up civil rights decisions of the circuit courts during the 1970–88 period. These data, reported in table 3.5, suggest that the rise in attention to civil rights cases during this period is anything but uniform. Most of the attention given to civil rights issues focuses on cases raising claims of employment discrimination. The frequency of appellate court decisions in this area likely reflects on dynamics in the political, social, and legal environment. Originally, Title VII of the Civil

TABLE 3.4.   Characteristics of Criminal Cases in the U.S. Courts of Appeals (as a percentage of criminal law/procedure decisions, by time period)

	1925–36	1937–45	1946–60	1961–69	1970–88
Drug offenses	7.6	3.1	10.3	17.2	23.9
Violent crime	6.6	14.4	23.9	31.9	27.4
Nonviolent offenses	65.8	41.4	38.2	19.9	29.0
Habeas corpus—Federal	10.2	17.0	9.3	4.3	2.1
Habeas corpus—State	3.5	12.7	15.0	21.8	21.4

Note: Drug offenses also include those that are alcohol-related, such as trafficking during Prohibition. Violent crime is defined here as any offense that fell within the FBI's Index crimes. They include murder, rape, arson, aggravated assault, robbery, burglary, auto theft, and larceny.

Rights Act in 1964 prohibited employment discrimination on the basis of race, sex, national origin, or religion; however, relatively few individuals litigated claims in this area until the early 1970s. Several factors may account for the sudden surge in litigation. Changes in society were occurring in the late 1960s and 1970s as evidenced by the civil rights movement and, more particularly, the women's movement. Increasing numbers of women in the workplace and heightened sensitivity to equality may have led more women to pursue claims of gender discrimination. In addition, Congress passed legislation during this time frame that would encourage litigation. In 1972, Congress authorized the Equal Employment Opportunity Commission (EEOC) to go to federal court to enforce the law. Other statutes were passed to provide more protection for women[6] and other disadvantaged groups[7] in the workplace. The passage of these statutes provided litigants with a cause of action, apart from Title VII, to pursue in federal district court. Higher volumes of appeals court decisions, however, also reflected uncertainty in this area of the law. Employment discrimination decisions of the Supreme Court throughout this time period settled a few issues but raised others.[8] Consequently, circuit courts heard a relatively higher volume of appeals in this area and devoted substantial attention to published decisions that would create circuit precedent for those cases with fact patterns left unaddressed by Supreme Court doctrine. For example, the circuit courts first held that sexual harassment of employees violated Title VII of the Civil Rights Act in the mid-1970s, nearly a decade before the Supreme Court issued its decision in *Meritor Savings Bank v. Vinson*, 477 U.S. 57 (1986). One leading case in this area was decided by the Third Circuit, *Tomkins v. Public Service Electric and Gas Co.*, 568 F.2d 1044 (1977). Tomkins brought a complaint against her employer alleging a violation of Title VII when her supervisor made sexual advances toward her and indicated that she would have to respond favorably if she was to continue working for him. The district court dismissed her complaint, but the Third Circuit subsequently reversed and became one of the first courts to recognize that the coverage of Title VII extended to this action.

The results in table 3.5 also indicate that civil rights appeals are frequently brought by prisoners, contesting the conditions under which they are being held. For prisoners, there are no "real" economic costs associated with litigation. However, these data also suggest that these appeals raised "real" legal issues as judges did not summarily dismiss their claim but instead wrote a substantial number of published decisions. Interestingly, desegregation cases, while they attract substantial publicity, do not make up a significant percentage of the civil rights decisions in the U.S. Courts of Appeals.

Civil Liberties Issues in the 1970s and 1980s

Over the last fifty years, judicial and legal scholars increasingly have focused attention toward court decisions that apply or interpret provisions in the U.S. Constitution that deal with fundamental freedoms of individuals. Since individual freedoms cannot be absolute and governments may, in the course of carrying out their responsibilities, infringe on these freedoms, disputes may arise that require the courts to resolve the claims by balancing the rights of individuals against the interest of the government. Most scholars examining civil liberties issues focus on Supreme Court doctrine; however, the lower courts play an important role in shaping the questions before the High Court. Supreme Court decisions are not self-executing; lower court judges must interpret and apply these decisions to cases where the mix of facts is not identical to the case addressed by the Supreme Court. To examine more closely the kinds of noncriminal civil liberties issues before the circuit courts, we analyze the case types associated with this general category.[9] The results of this profile are presented in table 3.6.

The text of the First Amendment guarantees freedom of religion, speech, and press. Given its wide coverage, it is not surprising that over half of the civil liberties (noncriminal) issues in published decisions from 1970 through 1988 deal with First Amendment issues. Many civil liberties questions were intertwined with statutory claims. In particular, a substantial number of these appeals concerned claims under the Freedom of Information Act (FOIA). In one of these appeals, *Patterson v. FBI*, 893 F.2d 595

TABLE 3.5. Civil Rights Case Types in the U.S. Courts of Appeals (as a percentage of civil rights decisions, 1970-88)

Case Type	Civil Rights Business (%)
Employment discrimination	31.2
Alien petitions	5.5
Voting rights	6.3
Desegregation	3.7
Section 1983	4.1
Prisoner petitions	27.7

(3d Cir. 1989), the court was called upon to interpret a section of the statute that prohibited federal agencies from maintaining records describing how any individual exercises rights guaranteed by the First Amendment. Other FOIA appeals frequently are coupled with First Amendment claims by members of the press seeking access to government records. Noncriminal due process appeals also appeared on the docket. Nearly half of the decisions relating to due process involved cases where litigants claimed that rights of access to the government had been denied or government employees alleged that they had not received a fair hearing or notice. A few decisions involved issues relating to constitutional privacy claims.

The profile of decisions by case type over time suggests that shifts in the issue agenda of the U.S. Courts of Appeals reflect on a variety of legal, institutional, political, and socioeconomic concerns. In the analysis that follows, we examine whether circuit-level differences (and similarities) exist in judicial business and explore whether these theoretical perspectives account for any patterns in issue agendas.

Judicial Business: An Intercircuit Profile

The data presented in table 3.7 suggest more similarities than differences in the circuits' judicial business. There are, however, a few notable observations regarding intercircuit variation. To begin with, the business of the DC Circuit is markedly different from the other circuits. As the primary appellate forum for litigants contesting decisions of administrative agencies, the DC Circuit's docket is dominated by public law economic issues (over 40 percent of their published decisions). Judicial oversight of executive agencies has grown over the past century with issues of administrative law often emerging in cases before the DC Circuit. For example, judges in this

TABLE 3.6.   Civil Liberties Issues in the U.S.
Courts of Appeals (as a percentage of civil liberties
decisions, 1970–88)

Case Type	Civil Liberties Business
First Amendment issue	53.0
Conscientious objector	9.1
Libel	7.3
FOIA (Freedom of Information Act)	15.0
Due process (noncriminal) issue	41.2
Privacy issue	9.7

circuit frequently have brought to the forefront questions regarding the extent to which the court should defer to the position of the agency. In a concurring opinion authored by Judge David Bazelon, "in cases of great technological complexity, the best way for courts to guard against unreasonable . . . administrative decisions is not for the judges themselves to scrutinize the technical merits . . . rather, it is to establish a decision making process that assures a reasoned decision" (*International Harvester Co. v. Ruckelshaus*, 478 F.2d 615, 652 [DC Cir. 1973] [conc. opin.]). A contrasting view was urged by Judge Harold Leventhal who argued that judges should take a "hard look" at the agency decision to determine whether the agency has exercised "reasoned" discretion that is consistent with legislative intent (*Greater Boston Television Corp. v. FCC*, 444 F.2d 841 [DC Cir. 1970]). In the late 1970s and early 1980s, the Supreme Court also addressed these issues, but the framework for analyzing these administrative law questions was initially developed in the DC Circuit.[10]

The notion that societal demands will influence judicial business is somewhat supported by these data. Appeals involving private economic concerns were more likely to appear in circuits dominated by commercial interests, such as the Second Circuit (which includes New York) and the Third Circuit (which includes Pennsylvania and Delaware). However, circuit-level variation generally did not appear to correspond to regions. For example, civil rights and liberties issues appeared more frequently in two circuits that are regional in character, but encompass different regions: the First (New England) and Seventh (Midwest) Circuits. Comparing the judi-

TABLE 3.7.   Judicial Business in the U.S. Courts of Appeals, 1925–88
(of published decisions decided by circuit, in percentages)

Circuit	Criminal	Civil Rights/Liberties	Public Economic	Private Economic
1st	24.2	15.1	30.3	31.1
2d	22.1	8.3	28.0	39.6
3d	18.8	9.9	30.4	39.6
4th	25.5	10.1	28.9	35.3
5th	32.3	11.7	21.6	34.4
6th	23.8	9.8	31.1	34.8
7th	21.9	12.6	28.9	36.5
8th	30.2	9.7	25.6	33.8
9th	29.6	11.0	30.6	26.1
10th	31.4	7.6	25.1	34.6
11th	32.0	23.1	20.0	27.7
DC	21.8	11.3	41.7	23.5

Note: Judicial business in the Eleventh Circuit includes cases decided from 1982 through 1988.

cial business of the southern circuits also leads us to reject the notion that circuit-level variation corresponds to regional variation. Nearly a third of the Fifth Circuit's agenda included criminal appeals. In contrast, only a quarter of the Fourth Circuit's published decisions dealt with the claim of a criminal defendant. Interestingly, judicial business was quite similar in two circuits, the Eighth and Tenth, both of which include states from several geographical regions. Earlier research suggested that the receptivity of a circuit to an issue type may be associated with the ideological mix of judges on the bench (Harrington and Ward 1995). These data provide only limited support for that premise as the First Circuit, historically dominated by Democratic judges, also devoted more attention to civil rights and liberties issues than the other circuits.[11]

Judicial Agendas and Sources of Law: Statutes, the Constitution, and Diversity of Citizenship Cases

An examination of policy areas through case types suggests that diversity characterizes judicial business in the U.S. Courts of Appeals. These issue areas shift over time and appear to vary somewhat by circuit. While these figures tell us a great deal about the policy context of decision making in the U.S. Courts of Appeals, this characterization does not adequately assess their work load in terms of the process of decision making or, more importantly, the significance of the precedent being created by the circuit court. In this section, we examine judicial business in terms of the sources of law to assess the extent to which courts engage in addressing issues raised by statutes, the Constitution, or state law (through diversity of citizenship cases) over time.

Statutory Interpretation

As noted by Judge Ruggero J. Aldisert of the Third Circuit, "whatever reservations we may have about the process, the proliferation of legislation has made statutory construction the essence in the day to day work of American judges" (1997, 284). Discerning the meaning of a statute has increasingly become commonplace in the federal courts as congressional legislation enacted during the twentieth century to address varying societal problems frequently leaves numerous "details" to be filled in by courts and administrative agencies. In the 1930s, Congress passed laws to establish New Deal economic regulatory policy, including the creation of administrative agencies responsible for implementation. Later, civil rights legislation and statutes dealing with the Great Society in the 1960s established federally protected rights. Additional regulatory legislation passed in the 1970s continued this trend. The passage of a statute does not automatically affect judicial business at the appellate level, however. As noted by Posner (1996), it is uncertainty surrounding the meaning of the statute that contributes to appeals in the federal courts system. For example, the large number of rights created by legislation since 1960 led to litigation in the courts as the scope of these rights was initially unclear.

In figure 3.2, the percentage of judicial business devoted to cases that raised a statutory question is plotted annually from 1927 to 1988. The line suggests a clear upward trend in judicial attention to statutory law beginning in the 1930s with the New Deal, falling slightly during the war years, and then moving upward in the 1960s with a fairly substantial rise beginning in the 1970s. In the New Deal era, judges frequently rested their decision on a statutory basis. During the war years, Congress did not pass many statutes that would require litigation in federal courts. The upward movement continued but spiked more dramatically upward in the 1970s. The increase in statutory cases likely reflects on the continuing litigation of claims based on statutes passed in the 1960s dealing with civil rights and welfare. In addition, the passage and enforcement of regulatory laws in the 1970s aimed at protecting consumers, workers, and the environment fueled litigation based on statutory law.

Constitutional Issues

To gauge trends in constitutional lawmaking by the U.S. Courts of Appeals, the percentage of judicial business devoted to cases that involved a constitutional issue is plotted annually for the same time period (1927–88) in figure 3.3. These data indicate that, like the Supreme Court, judges on the lower courts were more involved in constitutional issues over time. In particular, issues of constitutional interpretation rise substantially after 1970. At least a portion of this shift may be due to uncertainty created by the Burger Court as they began to issue decisions altering Warren Court precedent in a number of policy areas, most notably criminal procedure.

Diversity of Citizenship and State Law

While these data on trends in statutory and constitutional issues provide insight into judicial business on the U.S. Courts of Appeals, our profile

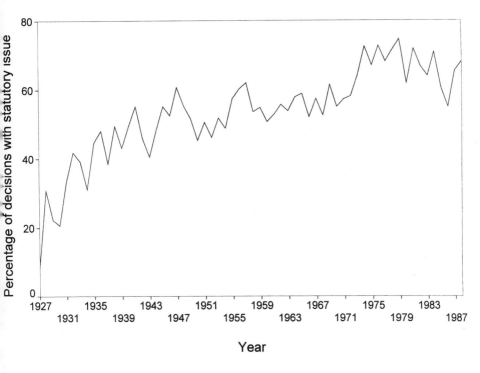

FIG. 3.2. Statutory law decisions (percentage of judicial business by year)

would not be complete without examining trends in decisions involving diversity of citizenship. In these cases, federal judges are called upon to apply, and possibly interpret, the law of a state. As noted by one federal judge, because state case law is rarely clear, diversity cases require judges to "engage in arcane efforts to guess what state law might be" (Coffin 1994, 64). Proposals to abolish or reform federal jurisdiction in diversity of citizenship cases have given rise to a large body of scholarship debating the merits of continuing to provide a forum where parties of different states may resolve their disputes (Low and Jeffries 1989). In general, those in favor of retaining federal diversity jurisdiction argue that in some areas of the law, there is not an incentive for state courts to consider the interests of large, out-of-state corporate defendants. Those in favor of federal diversity jurisdiction also have expressed concern over the quality of adjudications in state courts, particularly where judges are selected by election, and note the educational value of having federal-state interaction in our dual court system (Low and Jeffries 1989; Neely 1988). Reformers focus their argu-

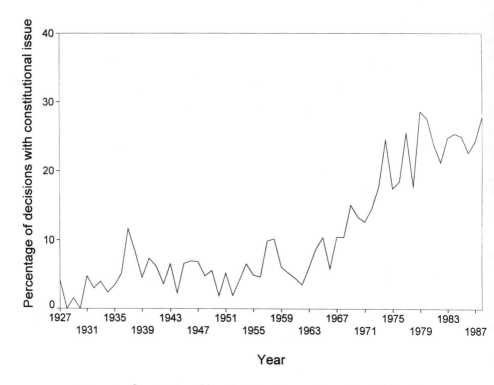

FIG. 3.3. Constitutional law decisions (percentage of judicial business by year)

ments on the need to stem the tide of diversity litigation in federal courts as federal judges devote substantial time to deciding and writing lengthy opinions that have little precedential value (Posner 1996; Low and Jeffries 1989).

While the debate over diversity jurisdiction continues (see Posner 1996), our analysis provides some assessment of the extent to which these issues have occupied the circuit courts over time. Plotting the percentage of published decisions that are diversity cases, figure 3.4 clearly indicates that attention to diversity cases in the U.S. Courts of Appeals has always been substantial, but that considerable variation has existed over time. In the early years, from the mid-1920s until the late 1930s, circuit court judges appeared to devote considerable attention to diversity cases. During this period, the appeals courts could apply federal common law rules to diver-

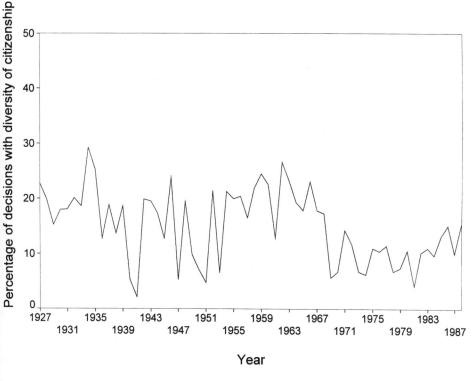

FIG. 3.4. Diversity of citizenship decisions (percentage of judicial business by year)

sity cases. In 1938, the Supreme Court, in *Erie, Lackawanna RR. Co. v. Tompkins*, 304 U.S. 64, held that federal courts in diversity actions must follow state law (both statutory law and case law). However, at the same time, the High Court established rules of federal civil procedure that created some incentives for parties to remove a diversity case and litigate in federal court. Our data suggest that the effect of the *Erie* decision was felt initially, but that in the next decade, appeals court judges continued to author opinions in diversity cases, possibly as a result of the need to create circuit precedent that would provide guidance on the rules of civil procedure. In the 1940s, the percentage of judicial business related to diversity cases fluctuated somewhat, and, in the early 1950s, these cases steadily grew as a proportion of the total. In the late 1960s, judicial attention to diversity cases in the circuit courts dropped to a level that remained relatively constant through the 1980s. Although Congress passed legislation changing the minimum amount in controversy required to litigate a diversity case in 1958 (and again in 1989), this change did not appear to influence circuit court attention to these issues.[12]

Conclusion

Our analysis suggests that judicial business in the U.S. Courts of Appeals is related to changes in the social, political, and legal environments, but that the strength of this relationship varies. Over time, the kinds of cases decided by these courts responded to change in society, but more dramatic responses to political and legal factors were evident. As part of the political system, the lower courts also must confront issues raised by the executive and legislative branches. In the past century, Congress has created numerous statutory bases for individual litigants pursuing a cause of action in the courts. Regulatory legislation, passed by Congress and enforced by the executive branch, also has contributed to a substantial number of issues to be addressed by the appeals courts. Still, the circuit courts' role in the judicial hierarchy also contributes to their issue agenda. Our analysis indicated that the kinds of issues addressed may be associated with actions of the Supreme Court that encourage particular kinds of litigation and appeals. Finally, institutional practices play a role in shaping the business of these courts. Unlike the Supreme Court, the organization and staffing of the lower courts encourage the development of formal and informal rules of procedure at the circuit level. These practices, along with other circuit norms, may encourage, or discourage, some types of litigants to appeal. Moreover, the geographical boundaries of the circuits contribute to issue specialization in the lower courts.

The perception that lower court judges are becoming increasingly active in statutory and constitutional interpretation is not completely without foundation. These data suggest that the issue agenda of the U.S. Courts of Appeals, much like that of the Supreme Court, is increasingly focused on public law issues, particularly those involving the application of legal texts from statutes and the Constitution. Moreover, these judges continue to influence developments in state law through their diversity decisions. Despite some limited efforts to stem the tide of diversity cases, these data indicate they have been and will continue to be a staple in judicial business before these courts.

CHAPTER 4

Parties before the U.S. Courts of Appeals, 1925–88

In the federal judicial system, the U.S. Courts of Appeals are the final arbiter for the vast majority of litigants appealing lower court and federal agency decisions. Although litigants may appeal decisions to the Supreme Court, the probability of gaining access to the High Court is extremely low. Howard (1981, 56) reports that in the late 1960s certiorari petitions from adverse appeals court decisions were granted by the Supreme Court in less than 2 percent of the cases. In recent years, the Supreme Court is granting even fewer petitions, while the dockets of the courts of appeals continue to increase in volume. The role of the circuit courts as final arbiter has been greatly magnified by these developments, and the importance of these courts as a forum for the "allocation of values" has been significantly enhanced.

In the previous chapter, we identified changes in the flow of litigation that have occurred in the appeals courts between 1925 and 1988. The appeals courts have seen their business shift from an agenda dominated by private economic contests to one increasingly devoted to public law disputes. The trends in the issue agenda reported in chapter 3 indicate a relative decline in judicial attention to private economic issues in recent years, while decisions raising issues in civil rights, civil liberties, and criminal legal policy have been on the rise. We attribute this shift in the agenda of appeals courts to social development and changes in the legal, political, and institutional context in which dispute resolution occurs in the courts.

While shifts in judicial business can result from environmental change, the decision to sue and appeal is solely at the discretion of the litigant. If we are to obtain a complete picture of the business of the appeals courts, we must examine the role of litigants in the appeals process. Modification of legal doctrine and judicial procedures, changes in social and economic relationships, and alteration in the ideological composition of the courts also may influence litigation decisions. In this chapter we focus on patterns of appellate litigation for different types of parties. Specifically, we are interested in examining which litigants are associated with increases in caseloads over time and whether there have been shifts in the propensity to appear before the appeals courts. Moreover, we explore the extent to which variation in litigation rates for party types reflects the influence of the social, political, legal, and institutional changes we found relevant in our analysis of the issue agenda.

After identifying who participates in the courts of appeals, we turn to the important question of whether increased utilization of these courts has resulted in changes in the allocation of benefits. It is often argued that the study of politics is the study of who wins and loses in the political arena. We examine winners and losers in the appeals courts to determine if the role of these courts has changed with regard to the allocation of values. Moreover, we look closely at the impact of litigant characteristics on decisional trends of the appeals courts across time. Our analysis draws on previous studies that indicate success in appellate courts to be associated with the expertise and experience of the parties appearing before these courts. We also seek to test whether litigant success in appellate courts is conditioned by changes in the litigation environment.

In recognition of the varying resources and motives of parties involved in litigation before the U.S. Courts of Appeals, our analysis categorizes parties as individuals, businesses, nonprofit organizations, substate governments, state governments, or the federal government. We examine participation and success rates of these litigant types across the five periods utilized in the previous chapter so that we may draw comparisons to our findings on changes in the issue agenda. An examination of litigant participation rates and patterns of success, combined with our findings in chapter 3, should provide a more comprehensive understanding of the changing and expanding role of the appeals courts in the federal judicial system, including any insights on the impact of social, political, and legal factors on the institutional development of appellate courts.

Who Participates and How Much?

During the course of the last five decades, the U.S. Courts of Appeals saw their work load increase rapidly to the point that some observers believe the institution is now in a "crisis of volume" (Baker 1994). While our purpose is not to suggest any remedies for problems created by the docket overload in American appellate courts, our analysis can provide an assessment of the types of litigants who account for the increased rates of appellate litigation. As part of this inquiry, we also are interested in gauging the extent to which changes in litigant types in the appeals courts reflect on broader environmental change. In the previous chapter, we suggested that environmental changes during the twentieth century had a significant impact on the agenda of the courts of appeals. We now explore the effect of those changes on the types of parties litigating in the appellate courts.

Social development theory posits that as societies become more complex and industrialization advances rapidly, there will be an increase in the tendency to litigate. Industrialization can lead to a new role for government in the area of regulation, which will in turn increase the probability of litigation between the federal government and regulated parties. Moreover, as societies become more urbanized and modern, the likelihood of litigation involving individuals will increase. In general, the theory assumes that increases in social complexity will fuel the propensity to litigate. Although social development theory is usually employed as an explanation of increasing litigation rates, it also provides some insight into the nature of parties involved in litigation. For example, in a developing society, increases in crime will lead to greater emphasis on criminal prosecutions, which in turn leads to more cases with individuals (defendants) pitted against the government. The advent of welfare in society can bring about increased participation by disadvantaged individuals seeking benefits. Changes in economic structures can alter existing relationships between businesses and government, which may lead to increased litigation between these two parties. Economic growth and expansion bring about increases in the number of business entities and closer interactions within the business world, which ultimately can result in higher rates of litigation among these types of parties. Technological advances in recent years have ushered in new types of claims in old areas of law, ranging from First Amendment claims associated with Internet use to patent and copyright claims associated with intellectual property. As a consequence of social development, old relationships are broken down and replaced by new and often more complex social interactions. The tensions and pressures associated with these changes can result in increased conflict and the need for dispute resolution by a third party. It is often the courts who find themselves in this role. The patterns of litigation in the appeals courts should reflect the dynamic changes associated with social development.

Political explanations addressing why litigation has increased over time center on issues of political access for citizens in American society. Studies examining the influence of political culture on rates of litigation find evidence supporting the premise that the use of courts increases when other political avenues are not available (McIntosh 1983, 1990). We know that some groups strategically seek out the courts as a forum for policy change after finding other institutions are not receptive to their claims. The courts have generally been perceived as a forum in which disadvantaged groups and individuals are able to find some protection from majoritarian rule. As other branches of government become less receptive to the interests of certain types of parties, we would expect those parties to turn increasingly to the courts to address their concerns. For example, the civil rights movement turned to the federal judiciary in the 1950s at a time when Congress and the president were less inclined to approach issues involving racial discrimination. In the early 1970s, women began to seek redress of discrimination grievances in the federal courts after recognizing other institutions were less hospitable to their claims.

As these examples illustrate, elected institutions at the national and state levels can affect patterns of litigation. The passage of statutes such as the Civil Rights Act of 1964 and the Voting Rights Act provided additional legal bases for disadvantaged parties seeking to litigate their claims. Conversely, the passage of legislation constraining the rights of individuals may lead to increased litigation challenging the validity of those laws as well as litigation enforcing the laws. In a representative democracy like ours, the political environment is fluid, a dynamic that reflects on the voting public and elected officials who, over time, may shift their support for certain groups in society. The extent to which these parties find other avenues of political influence closed and seek out courts to achieve their policy goals should be evident in increased participation in the appeals courts.

Policy-making initiated by elected officials also can influence the types of litigants in the federal courts. Responding to political pressure, both the legislative and executive branches have initiated policies aimed at reducing crime, an area of the law historically falling within the purview of the states. In particular, both branches of government have focused their efforts on drug-related crimes. Congressional legislation continues to redefine criminal acts and stiffen penalties. The administration pushes for the appointment of U.S. attorneys who increasingly have been aggressive in their prosecution of these laws. As a result, more individuals are appearing in the federal courts as a result of their being named defendants in a criminal case.

The nature of parties appearing before the appeals courts may be influenced by changes in the legal environment. For example, decisions of the U.S. Supreme Court establishing new areas of law can provide the legal platform from which parties can pursue litigation in the lower courts. Landmark decisions in civil rights and liberties in the 1950s and 1960s energized groups seeking the expansion of individual rights and led to increased litigation in these areas. If litigants do take cues from the decisions of the Supreme Court, we would expect patterns of litigation in the appeals courts to represent to some degree alterations in the legal environment brought about by doctrinal shifts. Parties also may look to change in the ideological composition of the Supreme Court as an opportunity to bring claims that previously had been rejected. During periods in which decisional trends of the High Court indicate less support for certain types of parties, we would expect those parties to be less likely to pursue appellate litigation in the lower courts. Specific decisions of the Supreme Court may facilitate participation in the judicial process. For example, in *Gideon v. Wainwright* (1963) the Court held that indigent litigants accused of a crime had a Sixth Amendment right to counsel and it was the responsibility of the government to provide that counsel if the litigant could not afford it. In *Bounds v. Smith* (1977), the Court ruled that prisoners must be given access to law libraries or other alternative sources that provide legal assistance to ensure their constitutional right of access to the courts was not denied. These types of decisions encouraged participation by litigants and provided increased legal access to the courts.

Changes in the legal jurisdiction of the federal courts also may affect the types of parties appearing in the appeals courts. One source of growth in appeals appears to be tied to judicial oversight of federal agency decisions. Between 1965 and 1975, Congress created twenty-six new agencies, so that by the end of the 1980s, the federal bureaucracy was issuing approximately seven thousand rules and policy statements per year (Carter and Harrington 1991). With the growth of the administrative state, federal courts have been called upon to review agency rules, adjudications, and enforcement actions. While some of these decisions are first reviewed by the federal district court, increasingly, case law and congressional legislation have established that appeals from the decisions of some administrative agencies should be directed initially to the U.S. Courts of Appeals. The appeals courts have also seen changes in jurisdictional requirements regarding patents and copyrights, diversity of citizenship cases, and habeas corpus petitions, all of which should affect the types of parties who appear before them.

Finally, the decision to litigate may be influenced by institutional considerations and strategic calculations as to the feasibility of appealing a case. Decisional trends in the appeals courts may serve as a cue to future litigants as to the probability of success in litigation. At various points in time the courts may be more receptive to the claims of some types of litigants compared to others. Higher rates of reversal in certain issue areas may indicate to litigants a heightened opportunity for successful appeals, while lower reversal rates would suggest the litigant should re-evaluate incurring the cost of appeal. Yet the extent to which litigants have accurate information about the likelihood of winning on appeal may vary. Posner (1996) suggests that over time there has been growing uncertainty affecting the decisions of litigants as they determine the likelihood of winning in the appeals courts. In support of this point, he cites differences in caseloads between the district courts and the appeals courts with the number of cases appealed growing at a faster rate than the number of cases filed in the district courts. According to Posner, uncertainty about appellate outcomes makes it difficult to negotiate a settlement below, leaving more litigants to appeal their case. Appeals rates may differ among litigants, depending on their ability to overcome this uncertainty. For example, individuals (compared to organizational litigants) may be less capable of making accurate calculations as to the odds of success since they have fewer resources and experience and may be motivated by factors other than economic considerations. The result is that they may be more likely to appeal a case that has little probability of success. Posner also suggests that increases in the number of appellate court judges in recent years has contributed to this uncertainty since it has become increasingly difficult to predict which judges will be on a panel and, if a case ultimately is heard *en banc*, what the outcome of the case will be.

Each theoretical perspective outlined above assumes increases in litigation are brought about by the influence of internal and external factors on the decision of litigants to participate in the courts. While they assume the litigant makes the decision to utilize the courts, the shortcoming of these theories (as they have been applied) is that their focus remains on overall rates of litigation, rather than on specific types of litigants. They assume litigation rates of all litigants will be influenced to the same degree by external factors. Conversely, it is plausible that increases in litigation rates in the appeals courts result from changes in the behavior of one type of litigant or a small number of litigants. It is likely that litigants base their decision to participate in appellate courts on various factors, many of which are difficult to measure precisely. Clearly, litigants have been more likely to pursue their case in the appeals courts in the last several decades. Who are the litigants responsible for this increase in the flow of appellate litigation? Has the nature of parties appearing before the appeals courts changed over time?

Participation Rates in the U.S. Courts of Appeals

To address these questions, we aggregate participants in the courts of appeals into six categories of litigants and analyze participation rates over the 1925–88 period. For ease of comparison, we utilize the five periods of analysis that were employed in our examination of issues in Chapter 3. The categorization of parties is similar to that used in other studies of litigants in appellate courts (see Wheeler et al. 1987; Songer and Sheehan 1992; Sheehan, Mishler, and Songer 1992) and includes individuals, businesses, nonprofit organizations, substate government, state government, and the federal government. The use of broad categories allows us to identify general trends in participation for different types of litigants. Participation rates are calculated as the percentage of cases in which a particular type of litigant participated in a given time period. Since our data consist of only those cases accompanied by a published opinion, we recognize that we may underestimate activity by parties who participate in a disproportionate number of cases that result in unpublished decisions. It is likely that this affects primarily individuals and businesses, particularly in recent years when the number of unpublished decisions has been on the rise. For example, we may be undercounting individuals involved in Social Security disability appeals, prisoner petitions, defendants' appeals from conviction, and businesses involved in the increasing number of diversity cases. These cases are more likely to be routine and will result in an unpublished decision. Data from the annual reports of the Administrative Office suggest that diversity cases[1] increased significantly between 1960 and 1980; however, we did not find a similar increase in our analysis of issues in the previous chapter, leading us to suspect that the publication rate for diversity cases declined during this period.[2]

The simplest method of evaluating participation trends over time is through a visual examination of the data. In figures 4.1 through 4.6, we provide charts illustrating the changing patterns of participation rates for each of our six categories of litigants. There are several distinct patterns worth noting in these graphs. Businesses (fig. 4.1) participated at a consistent rate until the early 1940s at which time they begin a steady downward trend into the late 1960s. There has been a slight increase in their participation rates since 1970, but they have not returned to the pre–World War II rates. In contrast to the trends for business litigants, individuals' participation rates exhibit a steady increase over time (fig. 4.2). The pattern of participation for the federal government (fig. 4.3) also exhibits a gradual climb over time but levels off during the 1960s and slightly declines since the mid-1970s. Participation rates have also increased over time for state governments (fig. 4.4), although the overall percentage rates are still relatively low. There is a substantial increase for nonprofit organizations (fig. 4.5) and for substate governments (fig. 4.6). The overall percentage rates for nonprofit and substate governments are also low compared to businesses, individuals, and the federal government; yet, over time, their rates of participation have increased.

Based solely on the data presented in the charts, it would seem that the parties contributing to the increase in judicial business over time are individuals and governments, specifically the federal government and to a lesser degree state governments. A clearer picture of who participates can be obtained by looking at changes in participation rates in our five time periods. In table 4.1 we report the percentage of cases in a given period in which a particular type of litigant participates as either an appellant or a respondent. For example, in the 1925–36 period individuals participated in 49.5 percent and businesses participated in 64.4 percent of the cases. We first compare the rates of participation across the five time periods for each litigant type. Consistent with the data presented in the earlier figures, participation rates for individuals shifted from 49.5 percent in the early period to 68.7 percent in the most recent period. If we compare this with the participation rates for business litigants, we see again that businesses have seen a significant drop in the percentage of appeals court decisions in which they participated as a party. What is most dramatic about this table is its juxtaposition of the individual and business categories, which demonstrates the role reversal that has occurred in the appeals courts for these two litigant types. Individuals have replaced businesses as the most prolific participant in the appeals courts, although businesses still participate in over 40 percent of the cases. Governments have also seen an increase in participation across the three time periods, with the federal government demonstrating the largest increase over time. Although state governments do not participate at the same levels as the federal government, it should be noted that their rates increased fourfold between the early period and the

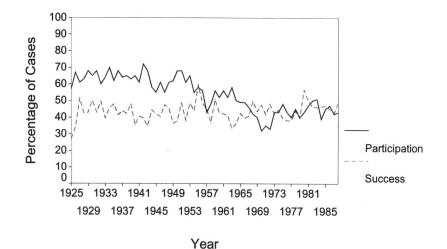

FIG. 4.1. Participation and success of business, 1925–88

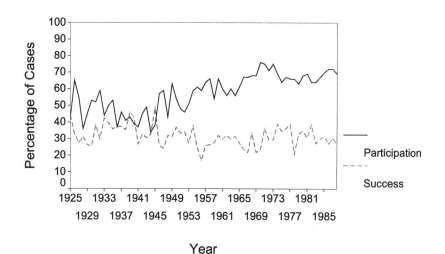

FIG. 4.2. Participation and success of individuals, 1925–88

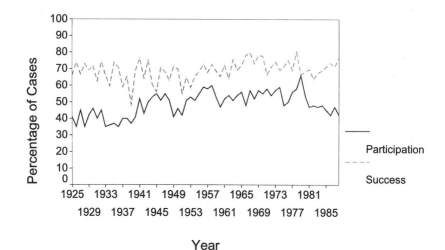

FIG. 4.3. Participation and success of federal government, 1925–88

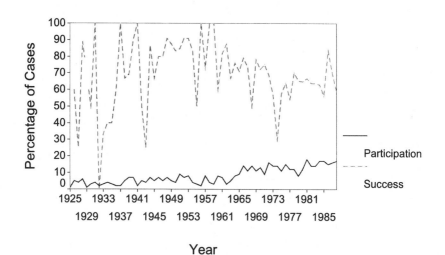

FIG. 4.4. Participation and success of state governments, 1925–88

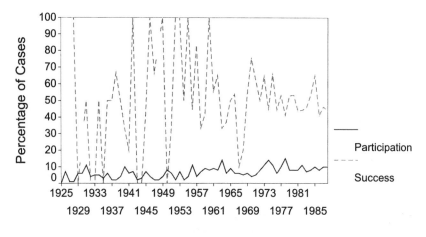

FIG. 4.5. Participation and success of nonprofit organizations, 1925–88

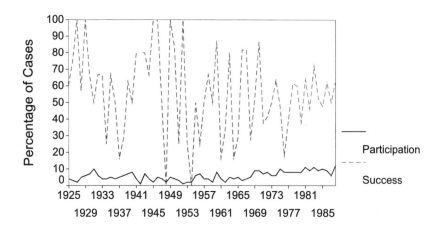

FIG. 4.6. Participation and success of substate governments, 1925–88

most recent period. Nonprofit groups and substate governments almost doubled their participation rates across the five time periods.

Examining the data within periods provides us with another perspective on changes in participation rates. In the early periods, the major participants were businesses, followed at significantly lower levels by individuals and the federal government. In the two most recent periods, the primary participants were individuals, followed by the federal government and businesses at a significantly lower level.

These findings suggest that the nature of litigation in the appeals courts has changed not only with regard to issues (as reported in chap. 3), but also with regard to the type of litigant. The courts of appeals are serving a different clientele in recent years compared to the early periods under analysis. Consistent with the findings reported by Baum et al. (1981), these data indicate that the federal courts have become a forum for the resolution of public law disputes. The dramatic increase in participation rates for individuals corresponds to our earlier findings of increasing numbers of decisions involving individual rights, liberties, criminal, and public economic law issues. In these case types, one would expect individuals to frequently oppose governments in appellate litigation. The increase in federal government litigation also reflects the growth in administrative and regulatory agencies in the last several decades. The appeals courts are increasingly addressing issues of administrative law ranging from labor disputes to environmental protection. An example of these cases is one originating in Kentucky involving the Clean Air Act (42 U.S.C. 7401) in which three Kentucky counties were not in compliance with the act's standards and were subsequently sanctioned by the Environmental Protection Agency. The Judge-Executives of the counties appealed the action of the Environmental

TABLE 4.1.   Participation Rates of Parties in the U.S. Courts of Appeals (by time period)

Party Type	1925–36	1937–45	1946–60	1961–69	1970–88
Individual	49.5	41.4	56.6	62.7	68.7
Business	64.4	63.4	57.8	49.0	42.6
Nonprofit	4.6	4.8	5.4	7.5	9.1
Substate government	4.9	5.0	4.0	4.4	8.6
State government	3.1	5.0	5.6	9.1	13.8
Federal government	39.1	45.5	51.5	53.4	51.4
Total (*n*)	1,916	1,510	2,501	3,001	6,671

Note: Participation rates are the percentage of decisions in which a party participated.

Protection Agency to the Sixth Circuit Court of Appeals. The appeals court affirmed the decision of the agency (*Dressman v. Costle* 759 F.2d 548, 1985). With increased regulation and oversight by federal agencies, the appeals courts are finding an increasing number of these types of cases on their docket.

Our earlier analysis also suggested that private economic claims were less likely, over time, to dominate the courts' agenda. In support of these findings, this analysis found participation rates for businesses had declined. Nevertheless, the sheer volume of cases involving business litigants is still very high. Our data permit us to estimate the total number of decisions in which businesses participated as a litigant.[3] In 1937, businesses were estimated as having participated in 1,555 cases decided with published opinion; by 1988, this estimate grows to 2,646. Businesses are still a major participant in the business of the appeals courts, but in light of our findings reported in the previous chapter, these results suggest that over time their involvement may include public as well as private economic disputes. Becoming more common in the modern appeals courts are cases such as *Russell Stover Candies v. Federal Trade Commission* (718 F.2d 256, 1983) in which Russell Stover challenged a final order of the Federal Trade Commission alleging violations of the Sherman Act. Increased regulation by the federal government has led to a growth in litigation involving businesses and the federal government. Nevertheless, the appeals courts still adjudicate a significant number of disputes similar to *Lange v. Missouri Pacific Railroad Company* (703 F.2d 322, 1983), in which an employee brought a negligence action against their employer, and *Para-Chem Southern, Inc v. M. Lowenstein Corporation* (715 F.2d 128, 1983), in which a company sued another to recover payment for providing a product. It is clear that businesses have seen the nature of their litigation change over time in the appeals courts.

Appellants versus Respondents in Litigation

The generally recognized right of appeal in the federal judicial system requires that the U.S. Courts of Appeals serve as the institution for entertaining a large volume of appeals. The increase in the volume of cases heard by the appeals courts is a direct result of the decision of a litigant to appeal a case. In effect, appellants determine the agenda of the courts of appeals, and any changes in the nature of litigation in the appeals courts will be brought about by the types of litigants who choose to appeal their cases. Respondents are passive participants in the cases and have no control over their rate of participation since they are mandated to participate by law. The overall participation rates presented in the previous section provide us with an initial view of the changing role of the appellate courts with regard to who is involved in litigation, but the overall data do not allow us to determine precisely which litigants are actively seeking out the appeals courts as a forum for adjudication. In this section, we analyze participation rates of litigants as appellants and respondents to determine if particular types of litigants have been more active in seeking out the appeals courts to resolve disputes.

The data reported in table 4.2 allow us to scrutinize the extent to which changes in participation rates are the result of active participation, as appellant, or passive participation, as respondent. In the previous section, it was clear that in recent years individuals have been involved in more decisions of the appeals courts. In table 4.2 we see that this increase in activity is the direct result of individuals seeking out the appeals courts as a forum for adjudication. Individual participation rates as respondents remain stable across the five periods while participation rates as appellants increase significantly. In fact, the increases we see in table 4.1 appear to be attributed to individuals' increased activity as appellants. This finding could reflect responses to changes in the legal context in which they litigated. Rates of individual appeals increase during a period that saw the Supreme Court deliver opinions that opened the door for claims of civil rights and liberties. The actions of the High Court also were accompanied by the passage of federal legislation in the 1960s providing individuals additional legal protection against rights violations. The 1960s also marked a period of time when Democratic presidential administrations were able to appoint most of the judges sitting on the lower federal bench.

The results in table 4.2 also indicate that businesses have been less likely, compared to other litigant types, to appear before these courts as either appellants or respondents, while nonprofit organizations have been appearing with greater frequency as both appellant and respondent. The decline for businesses is consistent with the findings reported in chapter 3 indicating that the docket of the appeals courts shifted from being dominated by private economic concerns to one consisting of primarily public law disputes. The increase for nonprofit organizations could reflect the modern-day phenomenon of the proliferation of specialized interest groups in the political process. As part of their strategy, interest groups have recognized the importance of the courts as a forum for policy change (and protecting the status quo) since the 1950s. For example, the successful litigation strategies of the American Civil Liberties Union (ACLU) and the National Association for the Advancement of Colored People (NAACP) in the post–World War II periods have been well documented in the literature.

Overall participation rates for states have increased, but table 4.2 demonstrates that those increases are the result of greater participation as respondents. States are not actively seeking out the appeals courts to litigate disputes but find themselves in these courts as a result of active litigation by other parties. This increase is primarily due to the increase in the number of petitions filed by prisoners. Another explanation for the increase in state activity is the expansive interpretation of the Fourteenth Amendment by the Supreme Court that has resulted in states increasingly involved in civil litigation brought by individuals.

The federal government is participating at a higher level as a respondent over time, while there has been a slight decline in participation as an appellant. The increase in participation as a respondent is at least partially due to increases in appeals by individuals. These appeals would include

TABLE 4.2. Participation Rates as Appellant and Respondent in the U.S. Courts of Appeals (by time period, in percentages)

Party Type	1925–36	1937–45	1946–60	1961–69	1970–88
Individual					
Appellant	35.8	30.7	46.2	54.1	57.1
Respondent	20.0	14.0	17.0	13.0	15.0
Business					
Appellant	49.7	42.4	38.4	32.1	26.2
Respondent	40.0	39.1	35.5	31.2	27.6
Nonprofit					
Appellant	3.2	3.4	2.8	3.8	5.7
Respondent	2.9	2.0	3.1	4.5	4.1
Substate government					
Appellant	2.1	2.4	0.8	1.0	2.5
Respondent	3.0	2.7	3.2	3.5	6.4
State government					
Appellant	1.3	1.0	0.7	1.4	3.7
Respondent	2.1	4.0	4.8	7.7	10.3
Federal government					
Appellant	8.8	13.1	12.1	9.5	8.2
Respondent	30.6	32.5	39.6	44.3	43.6
Total (*n*)	1,916	1,510	2,501	3,001	6,671

defendants convicted in federal trial court, federal prisoners filing habeas corpus petitions, individuals contesting the denial of benefits, and civil rights claims brought against the federal government. This finding also may reflect the increased role of regulatory agencies at the federal level. Finally, the low participation rate as appellant may reflect on case selection decisions of the federal government. In this respect, federal governmental litigants may appeal only those cases that they feel certain will be won on appeal.

The appellant/respondent comparisons in table 4.2 illuminate further the nature of the changes that occurred in the appeals courts with regard to who participates and how much. In recent periods, appellants are more likely to be individuals, and respondents are more likely to be governments. This portrait stands in contrast to the earlier periods when both appellants and respondents were much more likely to be businesses. Unlike the early periods where private economic claims between business litigants marked much of the business before the appeals courts, today's courts appear to be a forum for resolving a variety of disputes, particularly those between individuals and government.

Individuals and Government: A Closer Analysis

Our analysis thus far documents how shifts in the business of the appeals courts have brought about changes in the parties who appear before these courts, with individuals and governments more frequently involved in appellate litigation. Since individuals are appealing more criminal and civil rights and liberties cases (making the federal government the respondent), our analysis turns here to take a closer look at participation rates of individuals and governments. The results, displayed in table 4.3, confirm our suspicion that individuals participate at higher levels in criminal and civil rights and liberties cases as we move forward in time, whereas individual participation in economic and labor cases declines over time. A noteworthy finding is the significant increase in individual participation rates for criminal cases in the 1961–69 period. This is a clear indication of the impact of the Supreme Court's decisions on lower courts in the area of criminal procedure. The decisions of the Warren Court provided more opportunities for defendants to contest their convictions and for prisoners to identify legal claims in habeas corpus petitions. In the subsequent period (1970–88), participation rates drop slightly in this issue area, perhaps as a result of changes in the ideological composition of the federal courts. The growing conservatism of the bench may have curbed, either directly or indirectly, the numbers of prisoner petitions and appeals of criminal convictions. Similar to criminal cases, in the area of civil litigation, our data note a rise in individual participation rates over time culminating with a dramatic increase in the 1970–88 period. Even though the ideological composition of the courts may have been changing, individuals seem to continue bringing their claims in the decades following the rights revolution of the 1960s. We also noted earlier that these trends may have been stimulated by congressional legislation passed in the 1970s that recognized the civil rights of other groups in society, including disabled individuals and senior citizens.

State government participation rates parallel those of individuals with states participating at higher levels in criminal and civil rights and liberties cases while their participation rates for economic and labor cases decline substantially. Given the results reported in table 4.2 regarding their increased role as respondents, we feel safe to conclude that in criminal and civil rights and liberties cases they find themselves opposing the appeals of individuals. Similar to our findings regarding other litigants, in the early periods, states appeared in appeals courts primarily in economic cases, but when they appear today, over 70 percent of the time it is in civil rights, liberties, or criminal cases.

Over time, the participation rate of the federal government evidences a pattern similar to that of the states, with increases in criminal, civil rights,

TABLE 4.3.   Participation of Individuals and Government in the U.S. Courts of Appeals (by issue area and time period, in percentages)

Party Type	1925–36	1937–45	1946–60	1961–69	1970–88
Individual					
Criminal	20.9	28.6	32.2	48.8	43.0
Civil rights/liberties	2.7	2.8	8.0	6.8	20.2
Labor/economic	68.0	63.8	54.3	40.8	32.4
Other	8.4	4.7	5.5	3.6	4.4
State government					
Criminal	16.1	49.3	52.2	71.4	47.2
Civil rights/liberties	0.0	9.3	12.5	10.5	26.9
Labor/economic	73.2	37.3	26.5	11.3	19.3
Other	10.7	4.0	8.8	6.8	6.6
Federal government					
Criminal	28.7	21.7	29.8	44.1	45.4
Civil rights/liberties	2.8	1.0	6.1	4.5	10.1
Labor/economic	58.3	73.2	59.1	48.1	39.6
Other	10.3	4.0	5.0	3.4	4.9

and liberties cases and declines in economic and labor cases. The decline for economic and labor cases is not as dramatic as that found for the states, which likely reflects the continuing importance of the appeals courts as the first appellate forum for agency litigation. Nevertheless, the data in table 4.3 indicate that in recent periods the federal government has increasingly devoted attention to criminal, civil rights, and liberties cases. Like the states, the data reported in tables 4.2 and 4.3 suggest the federal government is increasingly involved in appellate litigation where the opposing parties are individuals.

Summary

Who participates and how much? We found that the answer to this question varies over time as the appellate courts have undergone dramatic changes with regard to their clientele. The original purpose of the modern courts of appeals was to alleviate docket overload for the Supreme Court and serve as the final stop for most cases. In the early years of our analysis, their role as final arbiter focused on resolving private economic disputes between businesses, or between business and government. During the course of the twentieth century the United States underwent social, political, and legal changes that redefined the role of government in society and contributed to a greater rights-consciousness on the part of the American citizenry. Individuals began to assert their civil rights and liberties to a much greater degree than in earlier periods of American history. Moreover, individuals resorted to the courts for enforcement of these rights. For some individuals and interest groups, forum shopping became necessary to seek out the arena most conducive to seeking policy change. While individuals were beginning to assert their rights, the role of government was also undergoing change. The rise of the administrative state and the codification of a substantial body of federal criminal law led to more disputes between individuals and government that, of necessity, were addressed in the lower federal courts.

For the U.S. Courts of Appeals these changes meant an increasing burden on the docket and a change in the nature of the parties appearing before appeals court judges. The case overload resulted in institutional reforms such as the splitting of the Fifth Circuit to create the Eleventh Circuit, developing procedural devices to process cases more efficiently (i.e., summary disposition), and increasing the number of seats on the appeals court bench. Overall, the rising caseload influenced the types of parties appearing before the appeals courts. In the last half of this century, these courts have assumed the role of arbiter of rights disputes, frequently between individuals and government. The extent to which individuals were successful in their pursuits will be explored in the rest of this chapter.

Winners and Losers in the Courts of Appeals

The question of who wins and loses in American courts may be the most important question we seek to answer as judicial scholars. Since the courts of appeals are the final arbiters in the vast majority of federal litigation, it is important to determine how different types of litigants have fared before these courts. Unlike the U.S. Supreme Court and most state supreme courts, the courts of appeals are mandated to hear all appeals from below and to perform the function of error correction. These institutional differences are significant in that they relegate the appeals courts to a role more akin to a referee of disputes between litigants. While appeals courts may decide cases that have important policy consequences, the majority of their decisions affect only the litigants involved in the case. This is quite different from litigants appearing in the Supreme Court, who wish to win, but whose primary interest lies in establishing a national policy through precedent. Litigants in the appeals courts are typically interested in overturning their conviction, vindicating their rights, resolving a dispute in their favor, and, more basically, reversing or affirming a lower ruling. If an appeals court decision brings about changes in the law, it may be an added benefit for the litigant, but it is not essential to their victory. It is this win-loss approach to each case that leads us to characterize these courts as institutions that play a direct role in the allocation of values.

In recognition of the importance of assessing who wins and loses in these courts and the apparent changes in patterns of litigation over the last several decades, we analyze success rates of litigants from 1925 through 1988. We are interested in determining the extent to which litigants who decide to utilize these courts have seen their decision rewarded with favorable treatment by the courts. Theoretical frameworks for approaching the study of litigant success frequently have drawn from the work of Marc Galanter (1974). In his study of trial courts, Galanter suggested litigants who are "repeat player haves" will be more likely to prevail over one-shotters in litigation. According to Galanter, repeat players typically have the advantage of financial resources and legal expertise. Moreover, they have the luxury of selecting cases that are more likely to be successful in litigation as they possess the time and experience to forum-shop for courts that will be most receptive to their claims. Although Galanter proposed his theory for trial court litigation, other scholars have tested the "repeat player versus one-shotter" or "haves versus have-nots" hypothesis in appellate courts. In a study of cases decided by sixteen state supreme courts, Wheeler et al. (1987) found the haves win more often than not, but the advantage enjoyed by the stronger litigants was a relatively weak one. Songer and Sheehan (1992) also found evidence of an advantage for repeat players/haves in their analysis of parties who appeared before four appeals court circuits in 1986. A study of litigant success in the U.S. Supreme Court reports little, if no, advantage for repeat players (Sheehan, Mishler, and Songer 1992). Collectively, these findings suggest that the advantages associated with types of litigants will vary depending on the forum. We would expect repeat player haves to enjoy a strong advantage in the courts of appeals because the lower appellate courts do not exercise control over their docket, in contrast to most state supreme courts and the U.S. Supreme Court. Courts with discretionary jurisdiction can choose the cases they want to hear, which leads to selecting those cases that are more likely to be reversed. Although litigants appealing to these courts are not likely to have their case accepted for review, if they do manage to make it on the docket, appellants will have a greater probability of success. Since one-shotters often are the appellants, their success rates will appear to be higher in courts of last resort than in lower appellate courts that are obligated to entertain all appeals, many of which are routine claims brought by one-shot litigants. Moreover, one-shot appellants in the appeals courts typically do not appeal cases that will impact national precedent; therefore, they are unlikely to garner financial assistance and legal expertise from groups who might have an interest in the outcome of a Supreme Court decision. To test these expectations, we examine the extent to which advantaged and disadvantaged litigants have been successful in the appeals courts and whether these types of litigants have seen changes in their fortunes over time.

Litigant Success in the Courts of Appeals

In our analysis of success rates of parties we utilize the same categorization of litigants and time periods we employed in the examination of participation rates. For a broad overview of trends in litigant success, we refer back to figures 4.1 through 4.6. These graphs plot data for participation and success rates for each litigant type for the entire time period under analysis.

It is clear from the charts that variation in success rates has not paralleled the trends we observed for participation rates. Individuals have seen their rates of success remain consistently low across the time period even as they were increasing their rate of participation in the appeals courts. The federal government has seen its success rate increase slightly over time, which corresponds to its increase in participation for the period. While businesses have experienced a decline in participation, their success rates have remained stable across six decades. The graphs for state government, substate government, and nonprofit organizations are very noisy because of the small number of cases. The numbers of cases for nonprofit organizations and state governments have increased in recent years so that we see some stability in their success rates during these periods. With the exception of the federal government, the data do not suggest a connection between participation trends and success. This finding suggests that litigants, particularly individuals, are not responding to evidence of success when making decisions to pursue their claim in the courts of appeals. It is possible that litigants who lose at trial, when contemplating whether to appeal or not, are not aware of the success rates for comparable cases or litigant type. Their decision-making calculus likely focuses on the facts of their case and whether they believe counsel can make persuasive arguments that will be supported by most appeals court judges in the circuit. Although we can only speculate on the reasons, our data do make it clear that the factors that influence litigant success rates are different from those that affect participation rates.

To further explore the success of litigant types we aggregate the data for the five time periods used in previous analyses. In table 4.4, we see only slight variation in the success rates of individuals over time, with individuals suffering a few more losses than wins in the most recent period. Businesses consistently won more than 40 percent of their cases over the five time periods. Nonprofit organizations increased their success rates over time to the point where they were more successful than individuals or businesses in recent periods. State governments' success rates experienced the largest fluctuations with a more than 20 percent increase in successes for states between the 1925–36 and 1937–45 periods and a 13 percentage point decline between the 1946–60 period and the 1970–88 period. The federal government maintains a high level of success across the periods, winning over 60 percent of its cases. Since the 1937–45 period, the federal government's record is particularly impressive—winning over 70 percent of the cases in which it participates.

If we compare the success rates of litigant types within periods, the data support Galanter's premise: stronger parties tend to prevail. Individuals were not very successful, and governments of all levels won over half of their cases. For the most part, these findings suggest an ordinal ranking of success rates that would reflect the influence of party status on outcomes in all periods. In the final two periods, the ordinal rankings are perfectly aligned with a repeat player/resources hypothesis. From 1970 through 1988, the federal government had the highest success rate, followed by other governmental entities, nonprofits, businesses, and individuals. These results are consistent with the findings reported in Songer and Sheehan's (1992) analysis of litigant success in cases decided by four circuits in a single year (1986).

Individuals and Businesses in the Appeals Courts

Individuals' participation clearly increased over time, but their success rates remained consistently low. To assess these trends more closely, we examine the success rates of individuals in table 4.5. It is possible that the low rates of success we observed in table 4.4, especially during the latter periods, could be the result of increases in the number of criminal cases involving individuals. Criminal cases typically involve routine appeals of

TABLE 4.4. Success of Parties in the U.S. Courts of Appeals (by time period, in percentages)

Party Type	1925–36	1937–45	1946–60	1961–69	1970–88
Individual	39.2	39.6	33.7	31.0	33.9
	($n = 1,020$)	($n = 637$)	($n = 1,548$)	($n = 1,941$)	($n = 4,407$)
Business	48.4	45.9	48.6	47.9	48.6
	($n = 1,601$)	($n = 1,104$)	($n = 1,747$)	($n = 1,708$)	($n = 3,156$)
Nonprofit	48.2	49.3	54.4	50.9	50.9
	($n = 112$)	($n = 73$)	($n = 149$)	($n = 218$)	($n = 556$)
Substate	63.5	58.0	65.7	61.8	59.0
government	($n = 96$)	($n = 69$)	($n = 99$)	($n = 131$)	($n = 520$)
State	50.0	74.0	78.2	71.3	65.0
government	($n = 60$)	($n = 73$)	($n = 133$)	($n = 272$)	($n = 859$)
Federal	68.8	64.6	67.2	73.6	70.7
government	($n = 701$)	($n = 625$)	($n = 1,267$)	($n = 1,578$)	($n = 3,205$)

convictions, habeas corpus petitions, post-conviction relief request, and other prisoner petitions questioning the validity of the conviction or sentence. These types of appeals generally result in affirmation of the lower court ruling and a loss for the individual making the claim. An example of these typical appeals is the case of *James Berick and Timothy Culver v. United States* (710 F.2d 1035, 1983) in which the appellants challenged their convictions on the grounds that the warrantless search and seizure, which resulted in the acquisition of illegal drugs and their subsequent conviction, was improper. The district court held that the one- to four-hour time period needed to acquire a warrant met the exigent circumstances requirement and ruled the warrantless search was justified. The appeals court agreed with the district court and affirmed its decision.

The rise of civil rights claims by prisoners also influences our findings regarding the success rates of individuals. For example, in *James Earl Buie v. Otis Jones, Sheriff; Frank Armstrong, Chief Jailer; Robert L. Hubbard, Jailer; Cumberland County of North Carolina* (717 F.2d 925, 1983) the state prisoner claimed he had been denied visitation rights while in a county jail for a temporary period awaiting transfer to state prison. The prisoner was serving a life sentence in state prison and was making no claim regarding his current incarceration. The Fourth Circuit Court of Appeals denied relief ruling that the appellant claim was moot since he would never be returning to the county jail. Additionally, habeas corpus petitions contribute to the large volume of cases that usually result in losses for individuals. These petitions are filed by prisoners who have been convicted in a trial court at either the federal or state level. Petitions filed from state prisoners must raise a federal question to be heard in federal court. For example, in *Futrell v. Wyrick* (716 F.2d 1207, 1983) the state prisoner filed a habeas corpus peti-

TABLE 4.5. Individuals' Success in the U.S. Courts of Appeals (by issue area and time period, in percentages)

Issue	1925–36	1937–45	1946–60	1961–69	1970–88
Criminal	29.0	33.3	29.1	20.9	23.7
	($n = 231$)	($n = 198$)	($n = 536$)	($n = 952$)	($n = 1,951$)
Civil rights/	31.8	37.5	40.0	29.9	23.7
liberties	($n = 22$)	($n = 16$)	($n = 100$)	($n = 127$)	($n = 850$)
Economic	45.4	46.4	38.6	42.3	40.4
	($n = 590$)	($n = 351$)	($n = 710$)	($n = 702$)	($n = 1,345$)
Overall	39.2	39.6	33.7	31.0	33.9
	($n = 1,020$)	($n = 637$)	($n = 1,548$)	($n = 1,941$)	($n = 4,407$)

tion claiming the admission of mug shots into evidence at his trial was a violation of due process and his Fifth Amendment right against self-incrimination. The appeals court held that the admission did not violate notions of fundamental fairness.

Individuals in criminal appeals are even more likely to have fewer resources and will not have accrued the benefits of a repeat player. Moreover, facing the prospect of prison, these individuals will mount appeals regardless of their merit. A typical example is the case of Julio Enrique Pineda-Chinchilla, *Pineda-Chinchilla v. United States* (712 F.2d 942, 1983). The appellant was charged with illegally reentering the United States and convicted in district court. He had been a party to an illegal arrest involving driving under the influence, but when background checks were conducted by the authorities they found he was illegally in the United States. Having no resources at his disposal he relied on the assistance of a public defender and filed an appeal claiming the immigration information should have been suppressed since it was obtained subsequent to an illegal arrest, that is, the information was "fruit of the poisonous tree." The Fifth Circuit affirmed the lower court decision in a brief per curiam opinion holding that the claim was meritless since the appellant had no proprietary interest in the INS file and therefore no expectation of privacy. This case demonstrates the resource differential between an individual criminal appellant and the federal government, but it also demonstrates the nature of many of the appeals filed by defendants. In many cases they are frivolous and trivial and result in expedient dispositions by the courts.

In table 4.5, the data suggest that overall individual success rates are reduced by the inclusion of criminal cases with the success rate in these cases dropping to a low of 20.9 percent in the 1961–69 period. Notably, this period marks the time during which the Warren Court was reshaping the constitutional landscape in criminal procedure with decisions such as *Gideon v. Wainwright* (1963), *Mapp v. Ohio* (1961), and *Miranda v. Arizona* (1966). Decisions of the High Court may have sent a signal to litigants that the federal judiciary was open to their claims, thereby fueling the propensity to appeal by individuals in these areas. Increases in criminal appeals apparently did not correspond to a similar increase in the number of meritorious appeals. The repeat player/resource hypothesis would suggest that, in fact, there would be little change in the status of the litigants or the quality of the petitions across time. Therefore, greater participation by disadvantaged parties just provides more opportunities for those parties to lose. In a study of the impact of *Miranda v. Arizona* on outcomes in the courts of appeals, Songer and Sheehan (1990) report similar findings, with litigants who appealed confession issues after *Miranda* seeing no change in their probability of success.

In the past thirty years, women have been more active in federal litigation than in any prior period. As scholars note, following the ratification of the women's suffrage amendment to the Constitution, active efforts by women to change policy were limited until the 1960s (Conway, Ahern, and Steuernagel 1999). The women's movement strengthened in the 1960s, leading them to push for political and social change. As part of those efforts, women have turned to the federal courts to address issues ranging from gender discrimination in employment to questions of reproductive freedom. In the appeals court, women were involved in litigation that emanated from several sources. Initially, statutes passed in the 1960s affecting the legal status of employed women contributed to claims alleging gender discrimination or inequities in pay. Subsequent legislation also protected the rights of pregnant women and attempted to establish equal access in education. Major landmark decisions from the U.S. Supreme Court, beginning in the early 1970s, established that gender-based claims

TABLE 4.6. **Success of Women and Men in the U.S. Courts of Appeals (by issue area and time period, in percentages)**

Issue	1925–36	1937–45	1946–60	1961–69	1970–88
Criminal					
Women	14.3	57.1	25.0	36.0	21.3
	($n = 7$)	($n = 7$)	($n = 16$)	($n = 25$)	($n = 61$)
Men	25.1	28.6	19.7	19.2	23.9
	($n = 167$)	($n = 161$)	($n = 417$)	($n = 852$)	($n = 1,694$)
Civil rights/liberties					
Women	—	100	20.0	30.8	51.3
	($n = 0$)	($n = 1$)	($n = 10$)	($n = 13$)	($n = 178$)
Men	27.8	14.3	47.8	26.0	39.9
	($n = 18$)	($n = 7$)	($n = 46$)	($n = 77$)	($n = 421$)
Economic					
Women	48.4	47.1	37.2	44.4	42.3
	($n = 128$)	($n = 104$)	($n = 148$)	($n = 151$)	($n = 274$)
Men	39.4	42.3	39.3	41.6	40.5
	($n = 363$)	($n = 213$)	($n = 428$)	($n = 454$)	($n = 749$)
Overall					
Women	42.9	48.3	35.6	41.5	42.3
	($n = 161$)	($n = 116$)	($n = 194$)	($n = 205$)	($n = 555$)
Men	33.9	36.0	30.5	27.3	31.3
	($n = 607$)	($n = 425$)	($n = 997$)	($n = 1,486$)	($n = 3,158$)

would be subject to heightened scrutiny under equal protection analysis. Decisions of the U.S. Supreme Court also firmly established Title VII of the Civil Rights Act as a legal basis for bringing employment discrimination claims. This trend toward successful litigation in the High Court should have laid the groundwork for increased successful activity in the lower federal courts, particularly in civil rights claims. In table 4.6 we compare the success rates of women and men in the courts of appeals. A comparison of overall success rates indicates women have been more successful than men in litigation. When we control for issues, we find that women did poorly in civil rights and liberties cases until the 1970–88 period when their success rate reaches 51.3 percent. For the reasons we suggest above, women increased their rate of participation in civil cases during this period and succeeded more often than their male counterparts. In other issue areas, women and men fare about the same before the appeals courts.

In the early years of our analysis, businesses were the primary litigators in the courts of appeals, and in table 4.4, we reported that business success rates remained constant over time. We explore the success of business further in table 4.7 with a breakdown by issues. What is most noticeable is the decline in success rates for businesses in labor appellate litigation in recent years. There has been a 16 percent drop in success rates from the 1946–60 period to the 1970–88 period. Success rates for business have remained stable in economic issues, and businesses seem to be most successful when litigating civil rights and liberties cases. Notwithstanding the decline in labor case success, businesses have been able to maintain a steady rate of success in the courts of appeals over the years.

Influence of Resources and Litigation Experience

The patterns of success described above would suggest that financial resources and litigation experience are important factors in determining the success of litigants in the courts of appeals. Although we cannot directly measure the presence of either of these factors in a case, we can make assumptions about the types of litigants more likely to be repeat players with access to greater resources. In our analysis presented in table 4.4, we suggest that the ordinal rankings of success provide some evidence of a resource/repeat player hierarchy. This speculation is based on our assumption that individuals in the appeals courts will generally have fewer resources than business and government. Moreover, individuals are less likely to have appeared before the courts in previous cases and therefore do not have experience in litigation, nor do they have the luxury to select optimal cases for appeal. In many cases the individual appears in court *pro se*, as was the case with Bill Williams in *Williams v. Goldsmith* (701 F.2d 603, 1983). Williams brought a Section 1983 civil rights action based on an allegedly unconstitutional search and seizure and requested permission to proceed in forma pauperis. The district court denied his request, and subsequently the appeals court affirmed on the grounds that his claims were frivolous. Although all individuals are not in the financial situation of Williams, most individuals are appearing before the appeals courts for the first and only time in their lives. In most of those cases they are opposing a government or a business, and they find themselves up against a litigant with more resources and experience.

In this section we examine more closely the repeat player/resource hypothesis as an explanation of success in the appeals courts. Other studies of appellate courts (Wheeler et al. 1987; Sheehan, Mishler, and Songer 1992; Songer and Sheehan 1992) examine this hypothesis with a net-advantage measure that allows the researcher to control for the tendency of a court to affirm and assess the ability of a litigant to overcome this deference to the trial court. In the appeals courts, the tendency is to affirm lower court decisions, so we begin with the assumption, ceteris paribus, appellants are less likely to win. Since individuals are more likely to be appellants in the courts of appeals (see table 4.2) it follows that they would have a low success rate simply because they are more likely to be the appellants in a court that tends to affirm the vast majority of lower decisions. The net-advantage measure takes this into account by comparing the success of a litigant as the appellant versus the success of their opponents (when the litigant is the respondent). The assumption is that they should have a higher probability

TABLE 4.7. Businesses' Success in the U.S. Courts of Appeals (by issue area and time period, in percentages)

Issue	1925–36	1937–45	1946–60	1961–69	1970–88
Civil rights/ liberties	50.0 ($n = 6$)	28.6 ($n = 7$)	57.1 ($n = 14$)	61.8 ($n = 34$)	51.2 ($n = 287$)
Economic	48.3 ($n = 1,111$)	44.5 ($n = 715$)	47.8 ($n = 1,141$)	47.7 ($n = 1,132$)	50.3 ($n = 2,056$)
Labor	35.7 ($n = 14$)	51.2 ($n = 43$)	58.7 ($n = 150$)	43.5 ($n = 216$)	42.3 ($n = 359$)
Overall	48.4 ($n = 1,601$)	45.9 ($n = 1,104$)	48.6 ($n = 1,747$)	47.9 ($n = 1,708$)	48.6 ($n = 3,156$)

of winning when they are the respondent compared to when they are the appellant. If their opponents are able to overcome the decisional bias of the appeals courts and defeat a litigant when they are the respondent, this provides evidence that they may be a weaker litigant. Net advantage is calculated as the *success of a litigant as appellant minus their opponent's success rate when that litigant is the respondent.* For example, the net advantage for individuals would be calculated as their success rate as appellants less their opponents' success rate when individuals are respondents. The lower the net advantage, the weaker the litigant in litigation.

In table 4.8 we report net-advantage scores for each litigant type across the five time periods. Individuals are consistently one of the most disadvantaged litigants in the appeals courts across the entire 1925–88 time frame. Moreover, when we compare the scores of individuals to governmental litigants it is clear that the advantage of government in litigation is overwhelming. While there is some variation in the ordinals with regard to government, for the most part, the net advantage scores are consistent with the premises underlying Galanter's party capability theory. The rankings are perfectly hierarchical for the 1961–69 period and the 1970–88 period, consistent with the expectations of a repeat player/resource hypothesis. Although individuals have increased their rates of participation in recent periods, they have been unable to overcome the bias in favor of government that likely results from being a repeat player in the courts of appeals.

Early studies of success rates in the U.S. Supreme Court identified one group of individuals who would be at the greatest disadvantage in litigation. Individuals who are considered underdogs in society are more likely to bring fewer resources and negligible legal experience to the judicial arena. In a study of the success of underdogs in the Supreme Court, Sidney Ulmer found underdogs increased their success rates during the 1903–68

TABLE 4.8.   Net Advantage of Parties in the U.S. Courts of Appeals
(by time period)

Party Type	1925–36	1937–45	1946–60	1961–69	1970–88
Individual	−11.7	−5.1	−12.9	−7.1	−17.0
Business	+0.4	−6.1	−0.6	−4.0	−3.6
Nonprofit	+1.0	+7.4	+7.2	−0.9	+5.0
Substate government	+20.5	+11.0	+6.3	+5.1	+9.8
State government	−8.4	+30.0	+42.9	+21.6	+20.6
Federal government	+21.8	+15.4	+15.6	+30.6	+33.6

Note: Net advantage = (success as appellant) − (when respondent, opponent's success rate)

period. In a reassessment of the Ulmer analysis, Sheehan (1992) reported that a reversal of this trend began in 1968 with governmental litigants defeating underdogs over 60 percent of the time in recent years. We identified underdogs in this analysis as individuals who appear *pro se*, who receive the assistance of public defenders, who utilize court-appointed counsel, or who can be identified as clearly below the federal poverty line. In table 4.9 we report the success rates for poor individuals across the five time periods. The overall success of poor individuals remains low across the periods with a significant drop in the 1946–60 period. This is followed by increases in the latter two periods, but overall success has never been higher than the 30 percent range. The pattern Ulmer observed in the Supreme Court is not evident in the courts of appeals, and the recent absence of support in the Supreme Court is more consistent with the treatment poor individuals are receiving in the lower courts. If we break down success rates by issue, we see that criminal cases account for the minimal success over time, with poor individuals appearing in civil rights and liberties cases only in recent periods. When they do appear in civil rights and liberties cases they have been more successful in the 1970s and 1980s.

Conclusion

It is clear from the findings in this chapter that the role of the courts of appeals has undergone significant changes in the last several decades. The courts of appeals were created to serve as a buffer for the Supreme Court by screening the increasing number of cases that had little national precedential value. In effect, the appeals courts were designed to be the final appeal for most litigants in the federal judicial system. This function has not changed over time, but the scope of this role has expanded dramatically. Rates of litigation have increased significantly during this century,

TABLE 4.9.   Poor Individuals' Success in the U.S. Courts of Appeals (by issue area and time period, in percentages)

Issue	1925–36	1937–45	1946–60	1961–69	1970–88
Criminal	14.3	27.8	13.5	21.9	25.1
	($n = 7$)	($n = 18$)	($n = 104$)	($n = 311$)	($n = 541$)
Civil rights/liberties	—	—	0.0	25.0	49.0
	($n = 0$)	($n = 0$)	($n = 5$)	($n = 24$)	($n = 98$)
Overall	30.0	22.7	12.2	23.0	30.7
	($n = 10$)	($n = 22$)	($n = 123$)	($n = 357$)	($n = 721$)

which has fueled the appeals courts' dockets. Various explanations for the litigation explosion have been offered to account for caseloads, including changes in social relationships, increased activism by individuals and groups representing individual rights, greater involvement of government in the economy, frustration with the accessibility of other political institutions, and shifts in the legal environment. Ultimately, though, the litigation explosion is the result of decisions by litigants to seek out the courts for change.

In this chapter we explored participation and success rates of litigants to gain insights into the influence of a changing litigation environment on the nature of parties in the courts of appeals. Our findings suggest that individuals responded to environmental changes by participating in greater numbers in the last several decades. The increased participation rates by individuals are for the most part consistent with changes that were occurring in the social, political, legal, and institutional environments. During this century, Americans became more aware of their individual rights and searched for institutions in which they could secure and maintain those rights. At the same time that individuals were becoming more rights-conscious and turning to the courts for assistance, the American courts were beginning to undergo an ideological change that would result in justices and judges more favorable to civil rights claimants. Decisions emanating from the Supreme Court sent signals to individuals that the courts may be the protector of individual rights against government intrusion. Statutes passed by Congress provided the basis for increased litigation in civil rights and liberties. Increased regulation by the federal government resulted in increased oversight of agency decision making. Consistent with our findings in the previous chapter, changes in the types of parties participating in the appeals courts were influenced by social development, but to an even greater degree by political and legal factors. The convergence of these environmental factors in the second half of the century changed the nature of cases appearing before the appeals courts. In the early years of the century, judges focused on those economic cases brought primarily by businesses. The modern appeals courts are predominantly hearing cases involving individuals opposing governments in criminal, civil rights and liberties, and public law economic issues. Businesses continue to participate at relatively high levels, primarily in economic cases, but they have seen increases in their involvement in civil rights and liberties cases in recent years.

While participation rates reflect changes in the social, political, legal, and institutional environments and therefore have been fluid over time, winning or losing in the courts of appeals appears to be a function of experience and resources, which is a more stable influence across time. There is strong evidence in our analysis that parties who are repeat players and have the benefits that accrue with that status and/or who enjoy greater financial resources are much more likely to win throughout the entire period we study. This conclusion is supported in the data when we control for issues and different time periods. Individuals have consistently low success rates while governments consistently have the highest success rates across time. Despite increased levels of participation by individuals and changes in the legal and political environment that were favorable to their claims, they still have been unable to significantly overcome the effect of party status in the courts of appeals.

CHAPTER 5

Decision Making on the U.S. Courts of Appeals

The rise of Legal Realism in the 1920s as a school of jurisprudence challenged the underlying premises of the traditional, formal model of judicial decision making. Subsequent research, led by C. Herman Pritchett's work on the Supreme Court (1948), provided empirical support to these views by uncovering patterns in judicial decision making that were not associated with the mechanistic application of legal principles. Over time, a substantial body of research now indicates that extralegal factors play a role in decision making for all levels of the judiciary, including the U.S. Courts of Appeals, where legal and institutional factors appear to mediate the expression of individual judges' policy preferences[1] (Howard 1981; Songer and Haire 1992; Songer, Segal, and Cameron 1994). Yet, a number of judges still adhere to the belief that the political preferences of judges do not influence their decisions. Judge Harry T. Edwards of the DC Circuit Court of Appeals argues forcefully that "it is the law—and not the personal politics of individual judges—that controls judicial decision-making in most cases resolved by the courts of appeals" (1998, 1364). Judge Alex Kozinski of the U.S. Court of Appeals for the Ninth Circuit is even more emphatic. He describes Legal Realism as a doctrine that suggests "that because legal rules don't mean much anyway" judges can reach any result they wish and can "engraft their own political philosophy onto the decision-making process and use their power to change the way our society works" (1997, 71). This is Judge Kozinski's appraisal of this "political" view of judicial decision making: "I am here to tell you that this is all horse manure" (72).

Given this continuing controversy over the impact of political forces on judicial decision making, scholars have tested for specific linkages between policy preferences and decision making, focusing on two factors that have been central to our understanding of the relationship between belief systems and American political behavior: partisanship and regionalism. Lacking direct measures of attitudes for judges in the lower courts, scholars have employed these as indicators because they are considered to be at least rough surrogates for certain policy preferences. As detailed below, their findings suggest that the influence of regions and party affiliation on judicial decision making parallels frequently observed effects of these factors on the behavior of the mass public and elites in the larger political system.

This body of research has gone far toward advancing our understanding of the relationship between judicial policy preferences and decision making. However, the behavioral revolution in the study of the courts is relatively recent. As a result, studies that examine the connections between judicial attitudes and decision making in the U.S. Courts of Appeals have been limited to court decisions from the 1960s to the present. We know relatively little about the bases of decision making before that time. The analysis in this chapter therefore extends our knowledge of the U.S. Courts of Appeals by examining judicial behavior from 1925 through 1988. As in earlier chapters, our analysis focuses on continuity and change in decision making for five broad time periods. After examining the extent to which dissensus has characterized case processing in the circuit courts, we explore patterns associated with political and geographical correlates of decision making over the sixty-four-year period.

Evidence of Dissensus in the Courts of Appeals

Analyses of the decision-making patterns of American courts have generally operated on the assumption that a substantial portion of the docket for courts below the Supreme Court has consisted of "easy" cases in which the legal texts are determinative so that judges, regardless of their personal preferences, will mechanically apply the law. In such cases, judges' policy preferences can be expected to be irrelevant to the decision-making process. However, judicial decisions do not appear to be constrained by legal texts in a substantial number of cases. A wide variety of analyses have reinforced the conclusion of appeals court scholar Sheldon Goldman that some cases present judges "with choice situations sufficient to alter the outcomes while other cases do not" (1969, 217). While there is no agreement as to precisely how many such "hard" cases exist (e.g., see Howard 1981; Songer 1982), it is reasonable to assume that judicial discretion exists at least in all "non-consensual" decisions of the courts. This lack of consensus is evident when at least one circuit court judge who heard the case dissents or the circuit court reverses the decision below. In either of these situations, the existence of disagreement among some judges would indicate that all of the judges who participated in the processing of the case exercised discretion as they determined which side should prevail. Thus, by examining trends in the proportion of "non-consensual" cases, this analysis will provide a rough indicator of the relative extent to which judicial discretion has existed over time.

The data in table 5.1 suggest that, over time, appeals court judges exercised discretion in about a third of the cases in which they rendered a decision. The rate at which the courts of appeals overturned[2] the decision of the district court or administrative agency below has remained relatively constant over the sixty-four years examined. The actual rate of reversal varied only from 26 to 31 percent, and even within this modest range there was no consistent trend.

In contrast, there has been a dramatic change in the dissent rate registered in the courts of appeals. In the first period examined (1925–36), the

TABLE 5.1.   Rates of Dissent and Reversal (in percentages)

By Time Period	Dissent Rate	Reversal Rate
1970–88	9.43	30.83
1961–69	6.67	25.66
1946–60	8.20	26.52
1937–45	7.07	27.68
1925–36	3.13	30.60

By Issue Area	Dissent Rate	
Civil rights/liberties	12.3	
Public economic	9.6	
Criminal	8.0	
Private economic	6.6	

By Circuit (ranked by dissent rate)	Dissent Rate	Reversal Rate
DC	11.77	35.82
3d	9.31	35.98
2d	8.84	33.76
4th	8.32	35.54
7th	8.07	28.46
9th	7.19	28.80
6th	6.94	30.84
5th	6.59	29.64
8th	6.32	25.07
10th	5.41	28.20
1st	4.49	31.52

Note: Data for the 11th Circuit include decisions from 1982–88; therefore, we cannot make comparisons with other circuits. During this period, we found judges from the 11th circuit dissented in 7.28% of the decisions; they reversed 36.26%.

dissent rate in the courts of appeals was a meager 3 percent. However, the rate doubled during the Roosevelt years and continued to climb through the 1980s to almost 9½ percent. To scrutinize more closely variation in the dissent rate, annual data are plotted in figure 5.1. While there is inevitably some random variation due to sampling error, the general picture that emerges from figure 5.1 is that a sharp upward break occurred about 1937, after which the rate of dissent remained relatively stable until the late 1960s. After the late 1960s, the rate of dissent began to climb again. If one were to take two-year averages to smooth random fluctuations, it appears that there was only one two-year period before 1937 (1930–31) when the rate of dissent rose as high as 5 percent. However, after 1937, there was only one two-year period (1950–51) in which the dissent rate fell below 5 percent. Since 1968, the moving two-year average remained above 8 percent; in the 1980s, that average remained above 10 percent.

Little previous work has explored possible causes of changes in the rate of dissent over time, and the data in figure 5.1 do not provide any definitive answers. Thus, our attempts at explanation are inevitably somewhat speculative. Carp and Rowland (1983) suggest that after 1969, precedent from the Supreme Court became more ambiguous, leading to a greater propensity for district court judges to express more openly their own policy preferences. If their thesis is correct, appeals court judges after 1969 also would more frequently encounter cases for which there is no clear, unambiguous precedent. This situation might be expected to lead to a higher level of disagreement among judges about the proper resolution of their cases and, therefore, a higher rate of dissent. The increasing rate of dissent noted for the 1970–88 period supports this thesis. Unfortunately, this explanation, as set forth by Carp and Rowland, does not appear to account for the earlier, more dramatic increase in the rate of dissent that occurred after 1937.

Searching for a cause for the earlier increase in the dissent rate still may lead one to focus on the High Court, as the increased rate of dissent in the circuit courts paralleled the rise of dissent on the Supreme Court. Analyses of changing patterns of dissent in the Supreme Court suggest that the Stone Court broke down the barriers of unanimity and legitimized frequent public expression of disagreement among the justices (Haynie 1992). This increasingly dissent-prone behavior on the High Court may have sent a signal to the judges below that such public expression of dissent was legitimate. It is likely that these divisions were fueled by the composition of the judiciary. During this time, judges on both levels of the courts had been appointed by a president, Franklin Roosevelt, who utilized judicial selec-

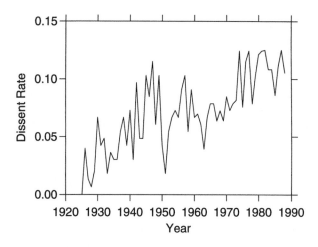

FIG. 5.1.   Rate of dissent in the U.S. Courts of Appeals

tion to advance the policy goals of the New Deal. The influx of appointees with specific policy preferences may have contributed to a judiciary that was more sharply divided along partisan and ideological lines. As we noted in chapter 2, Roosevelt's appointees to the circuit courts, in contrast to those selected by his predecessors, were more likely to be partisans with little or no experience as a lower federal court judge. Given their backgrounds, one would expect such judges to be more likely to dissent, particularly if the Supreme Court legitimized this behavior. The thesis advanced by Carp and Rowland also may have contributed to dissensus in the lower courts as precedent of a divided Supreme Court would be expected to add an element of ambiguity to the meaning of a number of the Court's decisions. In this situation, lower court judges could apply and interpret upper court precedent differently in the same case. While it seems unlikely that the reasons for the increasing rates of dissent in the 1930s on the two courts are unrelated, it is difficult to determine with any certainty if one or more of these possible explanations accounts for the coinciding trends in both levels of the judiciary.

Dissensus and Agenda Change

One possible cause of increasing rates of dissent may be rooted in changes in judicial business over time. We reported earlier that the proportion of decisions dealing with private economic issues declined substantially whereas decisions dealing with criminal law and civil rights and liberties increasingly occupied a prominent place on circuit court agendas. Decisions raising public law economic issues first surged in the 1937–45 period, then declined as a proportion of the docket, though at a slower rate than the decline in the rate of private economic cases. To determine whether these agenda changes might be related to changes in the dissent rate, we examined differences in the rate of dissent across the issue areas. These differences are presented in table 5.1.

Even a casual inspection of the data in table 5.1 suggests that there are substantial differences in the rates of dissent across issue areas. These results are consistent with the thesis that dissensus in the U.S. Courts of Appeals is related to the types of issues raised in the case. For example, the case type characterized by the lowest dissent rate (private economic) is also the only issue area that has steadily declined as a proportion of the total work load. On the other hand, issue areas associated with higher rates of dissent (civil rights and liberties) have increasingly occupied an important place on the appeals courts' dockets. Thus, it appears that the decline of private economic issues and postwar rise of civil rights and liberties cases before the circuit may have contributed to rising rates of dissent.

The findings reported in the third chapter also suggested that over time circuit court judges have increasingly addressed cases involving constitutional issues. Earlier research by one of the authors (Songer 1986) found that among criminal cases, those raising constitutional issues were more likely to produce dissent than those decided solely on nonconstitutional grounds. To determine whether these findings represent a more general characteristic of appeals court decision making, we compared the dissent rates in decisions discussing at least one constitutional issue with those decisions that did not identify a constitutional question. The rate of dissent in constitutional cases (12.7 percent) was significantly higher than the rate for nonconstitutional cases (7.5 percent). Thus, in addition to changes in the general types of cases, the increasing proportion of constitutional issues on the agenda of the courts of appeals also appears to be related to the rising rates of dissent.

Finally, the increasing tendency of the courts of appeals toward nonpublication may have substantially increased the rate of dissent among published decisions. Rules on publication generally suggest that most cases with clear precedent or that raise inconsequential challenges to the decision below should not be published. It would be reasonable to assume that such cases have very low rates of dissent. Therefore, as the proportion of the total docket of the courts of appeals without a published opinion has increased over time, the dissent rate in published decisions can be expected to go up even if the overall (published and unpublished decisions combined) rate of dissent remains unchanged.

Intercircuit Variation and Dissensus

Decision-making rules and norms in the U.S. Courts of Appeals are developed at the circuit level (Howard 1981; Walker and Barrow 1985; Van Winkle 1996). The circuits' varying regions and membership size also may fuel circuit-level differences in case processing. As a result, one would expect intercircuit variation in dissensus. To investigate this possibility, we examined rates of reversal and dissent by circuit (see table 5.1). Our results indicate that only modest circuit-level differences exist when comparing reversal rates. At one extreme, the Third, Fourth, Eleventh, and DC Circuits all reversed about 36 percent of the decisions appealed to them. At the other end of the spectrum, the Eighth Circuit reversed only 25 percent of the decisions it reviewed. Substantially greater intercircuit differences are manifested in rates of dissent. As noted in several previous analyses (e.g., Howard 1981; Songer 1986), the DC Circuit stands out as the most conflictual circuit, with split decisions in almost 12 percent of its cases. At the other extreme, the dissent rates in the First and Tenth Circuits were less than half the rate of the DC Circuit. Although the intercircuit variation in reversal rates was not dramatic, our data do suggest that the norms that govern unanimity encompass the two dimensions of nonconsensual behavior. Judges in circuits with high dissent rates also tended to have higher reversal rates, while judges were more likely to defer to the trial court judge in circuits where dissent also was less likely.

When the dissent rates of the circuits are broken down by time period it is apparent that the contentious nature of the DC Circuit is a post–World War II phenomenon. Before 1937, judges in this circuit court dissented in fewer than 2 percent of their decisions, and from 1937 through 1945, the rate of dissent was near the average for all circuits. However, since 1945, the dissent rate for the DC Circuit has remained steadily above 10 percent. In stark contrast, the First Circuit, which has the lowest overall rate of dissent, was actually the most divisive in the 1925–36 period with a 6 percent rate of dissent. Besides these two outliers, the patterns of most circuits follow the overall pattern noted above: that is, very low rates of dissent prior to 1937 are followed by consistently higher rates for all circuit courts, with the highest levels of dissent generally occurring in the 1970s and 1980s.

Partisanship and Appeals Court Voting

"To what degree do the political party affiliations of judges influence their decisions?" According to Carp and Rowland, this question has been asked many times, yet there is no consensus about the answer (1983, 25). Moreover, scholarship on the U.S. Courts of Appeals that addresses this question has been based on decisions of contemporary courts. We know relatively little about the relationship between politically based influences and judicial decision making over time. From a theoretical standpoint, a vast literature spanning the entire history of the empirical investigation of American politics has found a close and continuing relationship between political party allegiances and the behavior of both the mass public and elites on most issues in American politics. At the elite level, consistent differences in policy preferences have been found to exist between delegates to the Democratic and Republican conventions, between presidential candidates nominated by those conventions, and between both the leaders and the rank-and-file members in Congress.

Beginning with the now classic studies of vote choice in the 1952 and 1956 presidential elections (Campbell et al. 1960), scholars have repeatedly found a strong correlation between party identification and political behavior (Hill and Luttbeg 1980). While the causal connections between party identification, voters' positions on issues, and voting choice have been subject to debate, there is little dispute that the interrelationships among all three factors have remained high over at least the last thirty-five years (Hill and Luttbeg 1980; Pomper 1975; Markus and Converse 1979; Niemi and Weisberg 1984; Page and Jones 1979). Democrats are more likely to support the liberal position on a wide variety of issues when compared to the stances taken by Republicans. Finally, these studies also suggest that party identification remains relatively stable over time.

Research on Congress also provides support for the conclusion that party identification is related to policy preferences. A wide range of studies have found that "party remains the most important factor structuring the vote in Congress" (Schwab 1980, 196) or that party is the "best predictor of voting on the floor of the House and Senate" (Ripley 1983). Relative to other variables, including region and characteristics of constituents, party has influenced and continues to influence voting in Congress. The relationship between party affiliation and issue positions taken in voting on the floor of Congress has long been evident in the areas of government regulation of the economy and social welfare (Clausen 1973), but it is becoming increasingly common on civil liberties issues as well. Significantly, the direction of the relationship is similar to the relationship discovered in public opinion polls: Democrats are consistently more liberal on a wide variety of issues than their Republican colleagues. Thus, among both mass publics and elites, party identification is linked to policy preferences with Democrats generally more liberal than Republicans.

Apart from the need to examine the connections between judicial behavior and those dynamics that shape American politics, judicial scholars have focused on the nexus between party affiliation and voting for methodological reasons. To test whether judicial policy preferences affect decision making, one would ideally include models that draw on direct measures of judicial attitudes on policy issues.[3] Given the expectation that those who sit on the bench should be impartial decision makers who remain aloof from the political fray, judges are usually reluctant to discuss their policy preferences, especially as those preferences relate to the issues in the cases before them. Consequently, scholars have searched for readily available objective indicators that can reasonably be inferred to be related to judicial attitudes. Political party appears to be just such an indicator. Thus, scholars have investigated the relationship between judges' party affiliation and their voting behavior as a means of determining the impact of judicial policy preferences on case outcomes.

Overall, these investigations indicate that at least on the federal courts, at all levels, party is one of the best predictors of judicial decisions (Goldman 1966, 1975; Tate 1981; Carp and Rowland 1983; Songer and Davis 1990). Moreover, these results generally parallel findings about the relationship between party and voting behavior in Congress. Goldman's study, perhaps the first empirical analysis of the U.S. Courts of Appeals, found a significant relationship between political party affiliation and overall liberalism of appeals court judges (1966, 380). Since Goldman's seminal analysis, numerous studies have discovered partisan effects in judicial voting on the Supreme Court (Ulmer 1973; Tate 1981; Tate and Handberg 1991), the federal district courts (Carp and Rowland 1983; Rowland, Songer, and Carp 1988; Dudley 1989), and state appellate courts (Nagel 1961; Ulmer 1962; Hall and Brace 1989, 1992). A number of studies on the U.S. Courts of Appeals have reported significant differences in voting behavior that are attributed to partisanship (Goldman 1966, 1975;

Songer 1982; Gottschall 1983, 1986; Tomasi and Velona 1987; Songer and Davis 1990; Songer and Haire 1992; Songer, Davis, and Haire 1994).

The general picture presented by these studies is clear: across a wide variety of courts and issue areas, Democratic judges are more likely to support the liberal position in case outcomes than their Republican colleagues. A typical example of these differences is provided by the case of *United States v. Lowell Brown* (1988). As part of its campaign against child pornography, the Reagan administration approved a sting operation by the Postal Inspection Service. Lowell Brown, who was suspected of dealing in child pornography, received a letter from a fictitious corporation set up by the government inviting him to order videotapes of teen sex from a mail order catalog. Brown requested three tapes, but the government did not have any copies of them in stock. Not wanting to lose a chance to prosecute Brown, the government instead sent him a tape entitled "Preteen Trio" that was also listed in the catalog, but that Brown had declined to order. As soon as the unrequested tape had been mailed, the local U.S. Attorney obtained a warrant to search Brown's house for the video. Agents arrived with the warrant fifteen minutes after other agents, posing as postal clerks, delivered the unordered tape to Brown. The agents seized the tape that Brown had not viewed and introduced it into evidence against him at trial. Brown asserted defenses of entrapment and the failure of the government to prove scienter (i.e., the failure of the government to prove that Brown possessed a tape that he knew was obscene). The trial judge, a Democratic appointee, directed a verdict of acquittal, and the Reagan administration appealed. A unanimous panel of the Third Circuit Court of Appeals, composed of three judges appointed by President Reagan, reversed the district court and reinstated the jury verdict of guilty.

While these studies present systematic evidence regarding the relationship between judges' party affiliation and votes, most are limited in one important aspect. With few exceptions,[4] these analyses did not account for possible fluctuations over time. Consequently, theoretical development in this area has been hampered by a shortage of research that adopts a longitudinal perspective to examine whether partisan effects on judicial behavior remain constant across time periods. Research on Congress would suggest the need to pursue this investigation, as the relationship between partisanship and policy stances in Congress has varied over time (Brady 1973).

As a leading analysis in this area, Carp and Rowland's (1983) study of the federal district courts offers guidance for our efforts as these scholars systematically analyzed party effects over a forty-four-year period (1933–77). Overall, they found that 46 percent of the decisions by Democratic judges during this time period were liberal while 39 percent of the decisions by their Republican colleagues supported a liberal outcome (1983, 32–33). Across specific issue areas, Carp and Rowland noted wide variation in the degree of partisan differences. For example, in race discrimination cases, 57 percent of the decisions by Democratic judges supported the liberal position compared to 42 percent of the decisions by Republicans. Partisan differences also were apparent when comparing decisions where a defendant was convicted or acquitted of a criminal offense (43 percent liberal for Democrats; 30 percent for Republicans). However, Democratic and Republican judges did not differ very much in their support for the liberal position in decisions involving labor relations, environmental protection, rent control, and voting rights issues (1983, 38). The authors concluded that district court judges "seem to have split along 'political' lines more often on criminal justice and on civil rights matters than they did with other sorts of cases" (1983, 39).

Partisan differences in decision making reported by Carp and Rowland suggest that the magnitude of such differences varies over time as well as by issue area. Their data revealed that in the late 1930s and 1940s, partisan differences averaged about 4 percent, but "from 1953 to 1969 the difference between Democratic and Republican judges is very small with the "average difference between these two groups of judges a mere 1 percent" (1983, 35–36). Carp and Rowland found, however, that "beginning in 1969 a most interesting phenomenon starts to appear: the tiny gap between Democrats and Republicans widens to a sizable chasm—some 17 percentage points by 1972."

To explain the above results, Carp and Rowland suggest that the magnitude of partisan effects is a function of the degree of ambiguity of Supreme Court precedent.

> With the advent of the Burger Court, the trial court jurists could no longer count on the Supreme Court for as clear and unambiguous legal guidelines as they had received from the Warren Court's more stable majority. With the decline of the fact-law congruence after 1968 the trial court judges became more free to take their decision-making cues from personal-partisan values rather than from guidelines set forth by the High Court. Consequently the level of partisan voting increased markedly. (1983, 37)

While their conclusions are helpful in understanding party effects on decision making in federal trial courts, they may not be generalizable to appellate courts where the process of decision making is markedly different. Unlike trial court judges, whose efforts generally focus on fact-finding, circuit court judges evaluate claims of litigants regarding legal error stemming from the decision below. Circuit court judges also decide cases as a collegial body where appeals are generally heard by three-judge panels and, on occasion, all sitting appeals court judges in the circuit. To investigate whether similar changes occurred over time on the courts of appeals, we examined judicial voting in three general categories of appeals court cases that might be expected to produce partisan conflict. The areas examined were: (1) criminal cases, including state habeas corpus petitions as well as appeals of conviction in federal court; (2) civil rights and liberties cases, which included all claims related to the denial of the right to privacy, freedom of expression and religion, denial of equal protections, procedural due process, and rights guaranteed under the civil rights statutes; and (3) cases involving labor relations and/or government economic regulation. The five time periods used in earlier analyses were again used to track changes in party polarization over time. The results are displayed in table 5.2.

These results clearly indicate that partisan differences in decision making on the U.S. Courts of Appeals appear to vary over time. As noted above, many previous analyses of judicial behavior, drawing on decision-making data from the 1960s to the present, found a relationship between judges' political party and their votes in all three levels of the federal courts. The data in table 5.2 demonstrate that one cannot generalize about the magnitude of that relationship to longer time frames. Since the end of World War II, Democratic judges on the courts of appeals have provided consistently greater support than Republican judges for liberal outcomes in criminal and civil rights and liberties cases. While there has been some fluctuation since 1946, the results are roughly of the same magnitude as the average differences in decisions by Democrats and Republicans on the district courts, as reported by Carp and Rowland (1983). In criminal and civil rights and liberties cases decided in the latter time periods (1946–88), partisan differences ranged between 4.9 and 6.6 percent. Yet, prior to 1946, the picture is dramatically different. In both civil rights and liberties and criminal cases, Republicans actually provided marginally greater support to the liberal position when compared to votes cast by Democrats.

As noted in chapter 3, the specific issues comprising the agenda of the courts of appeals have changed substantially over time. Thus, many of the issues that produced partisan differences in earlier periods seem quite different from those that dominate the headlines today. Many of the civil liberties issues prior to the 1960s involved questions relating to extradition. Nevertheless, the same liberal-versus-conservative split was often apparent between the parties. For example, in 1954, two courts considered the nearly identical question of whether federal immigration officials were empowered to subpoena U.S. citizens as well as aliens and compel them to testify against themselves in deportation proceedings. In the first case, *United States v. Abraham Minker* (1954), the Third Circuit panel of three Democratic judges reversed the conviction for contempt of a naturalized citizen who refused to testify in a denaturalization proceeding brought against him. However, less than two months later, the Second Circuit, in the case of *Barnes v. Oddo* (1954) reached the opposite conclusion in a nearly identical case. The *Barnes* panel consisted of two Republican judges and one appointed by President Truman.

For labor and economic relations cases, the picture is more complex. Democrats provided more support for liberal outcomes throughout the sixty-four years analyzed, but the partisan differences varied substantially over time. Partisan cleavages are present in the immediate postwar period (1946–60), but immediately before and after that time period, party differences were quite small. In contrast to the earlier periods, voting by Democratic and Republican judges on the bench from 1970 through 1988 in labor and economic relations cases mirrored the pattern found for criminal and

TABLE 5.2.   Party Differences in Liberal Voting (by time period and issue area, in percentages)

Issue		1970–88	1961–69	1946–60	1937–45	1925–36
Civil rights/liberties	Democrats	33.5	24.2	23.7	22.2	23.9
	Republicans	27.1	18.6	18.6	22.3	28.2
	Difference					
	(D – R)	6.4	5.6	5.1	−0.1	−4.3
Criminal	Democrats	26.1	22.1	22.7	22.1	24.1
	Republicans	20.6	17.2	16.1	22.2	28.0
	Difference					
	(D – R)	5.5	4.9	6.6	−0.1	−3.9
Labor and	Democrats	58.7	56.7	55.1	67.6	57.8
economic regulation	Republicans	53.2	54.1	43.8	66.8	52.4
	Difference					
	(D – R)	5.5	2.6	11.3	0.8	5.6

civil rights and liberties cases. Specifically, support for liberal outcomes was 5.5 percent higher among Democrats than among Republicans.

Overall, these findings are in sharp contrast to those reported in prior research that suggested the relationship between party affiliation and judicial decision making would be consistent, with Democrats more likely to support the liberal position than Republicans. Instead, this analysis found the relationship varied over the time periods examined. While Democrats appointed to the appeals court bench have been more liberal than Republicans on labor and economic issues since the 1920s, the liberalism of Democrats on civil liberties and criminal issues is a postwar phenomenon.

One notable feature of the data in table 5.2 is that the pattern of change in the district courts observed by Carp and Rowland is not supported in our analysis of appeals court voting in three issue areas. Carp and Rowland (1983) observed that the gap in support for liberal outcomes between Democrats and Republicans grew dramatically after 1969. They interpreted this change as a reflection of the greater discretion available to district judges in the 1970s produced by an increasingly ambiguous precedent emanating from the Supreme Court. One would predict that such ambiguity would produce similar effects in appeals court voting. However, our analysis did not find evidence for this expectation, as differences in judicial voting by Democratic and Republican appeals court judges increased only marginally in the 1970s and 1980s. In civil rights/liberties and criminal cases party differences increase, but by less than 1 percentage point. In labor and economic cases, differences are greater in the 1970–88 period when compared to voting in the 1961–69 period, but the magnitude of party polarization is far less than that observed in the district courts. Moreover, when comparing across all time periods, partisan differences in decision making for cases raising labor and economic issues were strongest in the 1940s and 1950s.

Since Franklin Roosevelt's administration, presidents have been more likely to appoint judges to the appeals court bench that reflect on their efforts to advance partisan and/or policy goals (Goldman 1997). In particular, accounts of the selection process depict a process that has become increasingly politicized. Our analysis in chapter 2 clearly indicates that appeals court judges generally have been affiliated with the party of the appointing presidents throughout the twentieth century. To examine whether additional selection-based differences associated with each administration account for variation in judicial behavior, we compare judicial voting across presidential appointment cohorts. Because some presi-

TABLE 5.3. Percentage of Liberal Voting for Appointment Cohorts (by issue area and time period)

Appointing President	Civil Rights/Liberties	Criminal	Labor and Economic Regulation
1970–88			
Republican President			
Eisenhower	29.1	19.2	63.9
Nixon	25.9	19.7	52.6
Ford	27.2	21.2	47.1
Reagan	25.7	19.0	45.1
Democratic President			
Kennedy	35.5	26.4	60.6
Johnson	32.7	25.4	59.3
Carter	35.0	28.6	59.3
1961–69			
Democratic President			
Roosevelt	24.1	19.1	54.9
Truman	21.0	19.9	55.8
Kennedy	27.3	26.3	61.1
Johnson	21.0	19.2	56.2
Republican President			
Eisenhower	19.8	18.0	53.0
1946–60			
Republican President			
Coolidge	16.8	13.8	32.7
Hoover	24.6	21.7	47.9
Eisenhower	16.8	13.8	43.1
Democratic President			
Roosevelt	21.9	21.1	56.3
Truman	26.1	25.8	56.1
1937–45			
Democratic President			
Roosevelt	22.8	22.3	68.9
Republican President			
Coolidge	15.8	15.0	61.2
Hoover	23.8	24.5	61.8
1925–36			
Republican President			
Harding	17.4	18.1	—
Coolidge	30.7	29.7	49.7
Hoover	20.7	22.1	59.8
Democratic President			
Wilson	22.4	21.6	61.5
Roosevelt	46.0	48.3	55.5

Note: Includes only those cohorts with appointees who cast at least 50 votes in the issue area during that time period.

dential appointment cohorts are too small to permit meaningful analysis, table 5.3 displays the results only for presidents whose appointees cast at least fifty votes during the time period considered.

The trends in table 5.3 reinforce the conclusion that in recent years, party differences, rather than differences between presidential cohorts, account for a greater portion of the variation in the voting behavior of appointees to the appeals court bench. For example, in both the 1970–88 and 1961–69 time periods, the appointees of every Democratic president were more liberal in their voting than the appointees of any Republican president in both criminal and civil rights and liberties cases. In labor and economic cases decided in the last two time periods, the results were similar, with one exception: a small cohort of Eisenhower judges who remained on the appeals courts during the 1970–88 period appear to have been more liberal in their voting than judges appointed by Democratic presidents. Prior to 1961, the comparison among presidential cohorts of the same party becomes more complex. In each of the three earliest periods examined, there was considerable variation in the support for liberal outcomes among the cohorts of different Republican presidents. Hoover's judges were substantially more liberal than the judges appointed by either Coolidge or Eisenhower with the differences usually in the 8 to 15 percent range. Perhaps more important, the Hoover appointees were at times more liberal than judges appointed by Franklin Roosevelt. Comparisons among the appointees of different Democratic presidents are made difficult by the absence of many Democratic judges appointed by any president other than Roosevelt during most of the pre-1960 era. The one difference that stands out is that the Roosevelt judges were substantially more liberal than judges appointed by Wilson in both civil liberties and criminal cases. In fact, these data make it clear that the liberal posture of Republican judges reported earlier in table 5.2 for the 1925–36 period was primarily a function of conservative voting by Wilson appointees.

These data suggest that party affiliation appears to account for a substantial portion of the variation in judicial voting. However, the results in table 5.3 should not be interpreted to mean that differences do not exist between appointment cohorts of the same party. There are some notable cleavages. For example, Reagan appointees were more conservative in their voting on labor and economics cases when compared to appointees of other Republican presidents, particularly those selected by Nixon. It is possible that this difference reflects on their approaches to judicial selection, as Reagan administration officials made a concerted effort to appoint lower court judges who shared their views (Goldman 1997; Fowler 1984). On the Democratic side, the Kennedy cohort tended to be more liberal, particularly in criminal and civil rights/liberties cases, when compared to judges appointed by other Democratic presidents. This finding is particularly surprising in light of the observations made by scholars about the Kennedy administration's concessions to conservative southern Democratic senators in lower court appointments (Chase 1972). These data would appear to suggest that such concessions may have influenced the district courts, but did not affect Kennedy's impact on judicial policy in the courts of appeals. The results for earlier time periods also suggest some modest differences between appointment cohorts of the same party. Most notably, judges appointed by Hoover appear to have been more liberal in their voting relative to judges appointed by Coolidge, Eisenhower, and Harding.

Regionalism in the Courts of Appeals

As the intermediate appellate courts, situated between the nationally oriented Supreme Court and myriad district courts that are rooted firmly in their state political cultures, the U.S. Courts of Appeals have attempted to provide uniformity in federal law. However, with a decentralized organization, the courts of appeals have always been "susceptible to local and regional democratic forces" (Richardson and Vines 1970). The significance of place for understanding the functioning of the courts of appeals parallels the broader concern of scholars who have explored geographic patterns in American political behavior. As V. O. Key suggested, "in American politics the historical salience of place . . . colors both intellectual analysis and popular decisions. Our national politics has been regarded as the process of reconciling the conflicting interests and ambitions of the great geographical sections of the country" (1967, 100).

Key's insight is one that has been explored by numerous political scientists in a large body of research that cuts across the various fields of study in American politics. Underlying most research in this area is an assumption that the existence of geographically based variation is related closely to differences in political culture. Of the varying approaches that utilize the concept of geographically based cultural effects, the approaches that continue to dominate research on American politics emphasize the importance of regions and states for explaining variation in political behavior (Haire 1993). Underlying these approaches are two theoretical perspectives relevant to our study of the courts of appeals. From one perspective, public office holders, including judges, may be expected to reflect values and attitudes developed through "the shared historical experiences of people living in the same area" (Wenner and Dutter 1988). Another explanation for geographical variation in public office holders' decisions focuses on a more proximate relationship between the decision-making environment and the behavior of elites, including judges, who work and live in the same community with potential litigants and other interests who may be influenced by court decisions. From this second perspective, the location of the courts of appeals throughout the country should make them "susceptible" to environmental or contextual influences (Richardson and Vines 1970).

Since V. O. Key's early insights on regionalism in American politics, place-based differences in political behavior have been documented by a wide range of studies. Sharkansky (1970) found regional differences in public attitudes on race, family values, and international politics. More comprehensive research found that regional variation in public opinion on a wide spectrum of issues existed in the 1950s, 1960s, and 1970s (Wright, Erikson, and McIver 1985; Campbell et al. 1960; Pomper 1975). Studies of Congress have found regional effects in voting behavior (Clausen 1973) that existed even after controlling for party affiliation (Woll 1985). One leading scholar even concluded that region was second in importance only to party as a predictor of congressional votes (Hinckley 1983).

Given the attention to region in studies of Congress and public opinion, it is not surprising that empirical studies of courts have consistently found regional patterns in judicial voting. On the Supreme Court, Tate (1981) noted that justices from the South manifested more conservative voting patterns than their brethren from other regions. Similarly, Carp and Rowland (1983) found modest regional differences between northern and southern district court judges. Studies focusing on specific policy areas also indicate regional cleavages in decision making. For example, in his analysis of legal claims relating to segregation, Vines (1964) found southern district court judges with previous experience in state politics to be conservative. In federal court cases dealing with environmental policy, Wenner and Dutter (1988) found southern and western judges to be more conservative than their district and appeals court colleagues in the northeast. Songer and Haire (1992) also found southern appeals court judges to be more conservative than their northern colleagues in obscenity cases.

Although these studies provide some insight into regional cleavages in judicial decision making, their findings are limited in several respects.

To begin with, as we noted earlier, most analyses are limited to decisions of contemporary courts. Recent studies of congressional voting behavior indicate that place-based effects may change over time as North-South differences appear to be diminishing due to the realignment of the parties (Abramowitz 1980; Lamis 1988; Nye 1991). Although Tate's (1981) and Tate and Handberg's (1991) studies of the Supreme Court provide some insight regarding regionalism and judicial behavior over time, their findings may not be generalizable to decision making in the lower courts. Moreover, no consensus exists on how to define regions. While the most common approach is to employ a North-South dichotomy, there is some evidence that such a simple classification scheme may miss subtle differences that exist between regions (Sharkansky 1970; Wright, Erikson, and McIver 1985).

To explore the significance of region for appeals court decision making we adopted an empirically based definition that identifies four regions: the South, the Pacific Northwest, the Great Plains-Rocky Mountains, and the Northeast-Great Lakes (Haire 1993). The definitions of these regions were drawn from earlier research that employed a cluster analysis of state-level measures of policy liberalism, elite liberalism ideological orientation, and partisanship of the electorate.[5] The proportions of liberal votes cast by judges sitting on the bench in each of these four regions were then computed for the five time periods used in the earlier analysis of partisan differences. Since prior research notes that the influence of region may vary by issue area, we analyze regional effects for three case types: civil rights/liberties, criminal, and labor and economic cases. The results are displayed in table 5.4.

At one level, the data in table 5.4 support the findings of earlier studies that found regional differences in judicial voting on all three levels of the federal courts. For all issue areas examined, regional differences were manifested in each time period. Yet, the most striking finding was that the significance of region for judicial voting on the courts of appeals has changed dramatically over time. In all three issue areas, regional differences were strongest in the 1925–36 time period, but have diminished with the passage of time. In cases involving labor and economic regulation issues, regional differences almost disappeared by the 1970–88 period, as support for liberal outcomes varied from 58.0 percent in the Pacific Northwest to 55.6 percent in the South, a difference of only 2.4 percent. While modest regional differences remained in criminal and civil rights and liberties decisions in the 1970s and 1980s, the magnitude of those differences had declined precipitously from the 1920s and 1930s. In civil rights and liberties claims, the range of regional differences in support for liberal outcomes varied from 22.3 percent in the 1925–36 period to a mere 5.7 percent in 1970 through 1988. Similarly, in criminal cases, the regional differential of 29.2 percent observed in 1925–36 had dropped to only 6.4 percent in the 1970–88 period.

These findings also suggested that the common practice of using a simple South/non-south dichotomy may not be adequate for understanding place-based variation. The notion of a distinctive southern region characterized by conservative policy preferences was not fully supported by data on decision making in the courts of appeals. While the South was frequently more conservative than the average of the other three regions, it is not uniformly so. More importantly, the South was not consistently the most conservative region in any of the three issue areas. It was the most conservative region in only one period for each of the issue areas (1925–36 for civil rights/ liberties and criminal cases; 1937–45 for labor and economic cases). In most periods, it was not at either extreme. There were a few periods and case types in which southern appeals court judges were the most liberal: labor and economics cases decided from 1925 through 1936 and civil rights and liberties cases decided from 1946 through 1960.

TABLE 5.4.   Regional Differences in Liberal Voting (by time period and issue area, in percentages)

Issue	Region	1970–88	1961–69	1946–60	1937–45	1925–36
Civil rights/liberties	South	28.9	20.7	24.7	18.3	18.7
	Great Plains	26.7	18.3	10.5	36.1	25.5
	Pacific	31.4	13.7	17.1	16.9	41.0
	Northeast/Great Lakes	32.4	23.8	23.4	21.6	31.8
	Difference	5.7	10.1	14.2	19.2	22.3
Criminal	South	22.6	18.6	21.9	17.6	16.6
	Great Plains	19.1	18.2	9.9	36.8	27.5
	Pacific	24.0	13.1	16.0	16.9	45.8
	Northeast/Great Lakes	25.5	21.2	22.0	21.2	31.5
	Difference	6.4	8.1	12.1	19.9	29.2
Labor and economic regulation	South	55.6	57.3	49.9	64.3	59.3
	Great Plains	55.6	51.3	57.7	69.1	45.1
	Pacific	58.0	62.5	60.7	78.0	53.3
	Northeast/Great Lakes	56.6	53.8	48.1	67.5	50.6
	Difference	2.4	11.2	12.6	13.7	14.2

Note: Difference figure is calculated by subtracting the percentage liberal for most liberal region from the percentage liberal for most conservative region.

Although decisions from judges in the South did not tend to be conservative, voting by judges in the Northeast-Great Lakes area tended to be more liberal in criminal and civil rights and liberties cases decided since 1946. Voting by judges in the Pacific-West Coast in labor and economics cases also was distinctively liberal in most of the time periods examined.

Before we disregard the notion of southern distinctiveness and draw even tentative conclusions about regionalism in decision making on the appeals courts, it is necessary to consider the possible confounding effects of party affiliation. Our earlier findings, reported in tables 5.2 and 5.3, suggested that Democratic judges were more liberal than Republican judges, particularly since the postwar period. Therefore, the variation in regional effects noted in table 5.4 may be due to changes over time as the partisan balance on the bench shifted to reflect turnover in the judiciary. To control for this possibility, we utilized a multivariate model to test for the effects of both party and region on judicial voting in each time period. The dependent variable (judges' votes) was coded 1 if the vote supported the liberal position and 0 for votes that supported the conservative position. Votes that could not be unambiguously classified as liberal or conservative were excluded from analysis. Party affiliation was coded 1 if the judge was affiliated with the Democratic party and 0 if the judge was a Republican. A series of dummy variables was utilized to identify whether the case was decided in one of the four regions identified above. In the analysis reported below, the excluded ("reference") region was the South.

Since our dependent variable is dichotomous, the parameters are estimated by logistic regression, a maximum likelihood estimation technique (Aldrich and Nelson 1984). This method produces estimates for the parameters of the model's independent variables in terms of the contribution each makes to the probability that the dependent variable falls into one of the two designated categories (either a liberal or a conservative vote). For each independent variable, a maximum likelihood estimate (MLE) is calculated along with its standard error. The MLEs represent the change in the logistic function that results from a one-unit change in the independent variable. A test of significance is computed for each coefficient in the logistic regression model using the MLE and its standard error. The results of these models are compiled in table 5.5.

The data in table 5.5 summarize the results of fifteen different models. Since the coefficients of the maximum likelihood estimates produced by logistic regression are not easily interpretable, we present in table 5.5 the odds ratios for each of the variables that were related to the probability of a liberal vote to a statistically significant degree. The odds ratio measures the proportionate change in the dependent variable that coincides with a single unit difference on the independent variable. Values over 1.0 for the party variable show that the odds of a liberal vote are greater for Democratic than Republican judges when region is held constant. For example, the odds ratio of 1.32 reported in the second column of table 5.5 indicates that the odds of a Democratic judge casting a liberal vote are 1.32 times greater than the odds of a Republican judge from the same region casting such a liberal vote in criminal cases in the 1970–88 period. The results regarding the effect of judicial party affiliation generally affirm the results of the bivariate analysis presented earlier. For criminal and civil rights and liberties cases, Democratic judges were more likely than Republicans to cast liberal votes in each period after the end of World War II, even after controlling for region. However, prior to that time, party differences were not statistically significant. For labor and economic cases, the results suggest the same pattern observed without regional controls. That is, party differences were strongest in the 1946–60 period, but were not significant immediately before and after this time. In the earliest (1925–36) and most recent (1970–88) periods, party differences in decision making dealing with labor and economics claims were modest, but statistically significant.

The results presented in table 5.5 again suggest a somewhat mixed picture regarding regional effects. After controlling for party, our regional

TABLE 5.5. Odds Ratios for Statistically Significant Relationships: Estimated Effects of Party and Region (by time period and issue area)

	1970–88	1961–69	1946–60	1937–45	1925–36
Civil rights/liberties					
Democrat	1.32	1.30	1.38	—	—
Pacific		0.57	0.58	—	2.14
Great Plains	0.79[a]	0.33	2.48	—	
Northeast/Great Lakes	1.09[a]	—	0.79[a]	—	1.53
Criminal					
Democrat	1.32	1.29	1.54	—	—
Pacific		0.61	0.57	—	2.62
Great Plains	0.82	—	2.63	—	—
Northeast/Great Lakes	—	—	—	—	1.60
Labor and economic regulation					
Democrat	1.23	—	1.57	—	1.19
Pacific	—	—	—	—	—
Great Plains	—	0.77[a]	—	—	0.59
Northeast/Great Lakes	—	0.86	—	—	0.72

Note: The excluded, reference category is the South.
[a]Significant at .10 level; other values of odds ratios significant at .05 level.

cleavages presented in the bivariate analysis also appear to hold here. However, our model focuses on testing for southern distinctiveness and, for this reason, presents more insight on this question. In criminal and civil rights and liberties cases, judges in the South appear to vote in a distinctive pattern; however, this relationship shifts after World War II. Prior to 1946, judges in the South tended to be more conservative in their voting on criminal and civil rights/liberties cases than judges from many of the other regions. However, since that time, voting by southern judges in these issue areas appears to be characterized by moderation. In fact, relative to their colleagues in the South, appeals court judges in the Great Plains-Rocky Mountains region appear to be the most conservative, as they voted more frequently against the claims of the criminal defendant in the 1970–88 period and more frequently against the civil rights/liberties claim in the two periods immediately following World War II (1946–69). A similar pattern is noted for judges from the Pacific Northwest in the 1946–60 and 1961–69 periods. Relative to the voting of judges from the South, judges in this region were less likely to support the liberal position in criminal and civil rights and liberties cases to a statistically significant degree. The results from our bivariate analysis found that regionalism did not explain very well decision making in labor and economic cases. Our analysis utilizing multivariate models also supports that impression. The only statistically significant regional cleavages in these models were found in the first (1925–36) and fourth (1961–69) periods. During these periods, judicial voting in the Northeast-Great Lakes and Great Plains regions was more conservative than in the South.

The addition of a control for judges' political party reaffirms the conclusion based on the earlier analysis that the South is not a distinctively conservative region, particularly since the end of World War II. To the extent that regional cleavages were found, they varied over time. Thus, these results support our earlier impression that the meaning of region for judicial politics is not constant across time. A further indication of the change over time is that the Great Plains-Rocky Mountains region, the most conservative region overall in the postwar period, is actually the most liberal region for civil liberties cases in the 1937–45 period.

Regionalism and Circuit Boundaries

Most analyses of geographical patterns of behavior in American courts, like the one above, have focused on region. But there are good theoretical reasons for guessing that variation in court outcomes across the country may have more to do with circuits than regions (Haire 1993). From the perspective of communications theory, the "circuit is a semi-closed system, a system within which there is considerable interaction among its members and almost no interaction between the members of one system (circuit) and another" (Carp 1972, 472). Moreover, given the norm to adhere to stare decisis and the interest in uniformity within the circuit, one would expect circuit law to guide judicial decisions for appellate judges within the circuit. Thus, it is not surprising that several studies of judicial voting have found intercircuit differences in several areas of law (Howard 1981; Goldman 1975). Empirical studies of intercircuit differences, unfortunately, are relatively rare and frequently attribute such differences to influences associated with regionalism (Howard 1981; Wenner and Dutter 1988). On the other hand, a reanalysis of Howard's conclusions regarding regional differences in agenda setting discovered that circuits rather than regions were the most important sources of variation (Davis and Songer 1989). In the district courts, Carp and Rowland (1983) noted that differences among circuits in support for liberal outcomes is of approximately the same magnitude as differences among regions. In addition, their data indicate that in some time periods the differences among circuits within a region are as great as the average differences between the regions. Similarly, Haire (1993) found that intercircuit differences persisted in appeals court voting behavior even after controlling for the effects of region.

To provide a rough approximation of the relative significance of regions versus circuits for appeals court outcomes, we compared the differences in the proportion of liberal votes cast by judges within the same region but in different circuits with the differences among regions discussed above. The results are displayed in table 5.6.

The first complication in such a comparison is that circuit lines do not always fall neatly along regional lines. Most obviously, the Sixth Circuit, stretching from Tennessee to the Great Lakes, and the Eighth Circuit, covering territory from Arkansas to the Canadian border, cannot be categorized as being part of any single region. At the other end of the spectrum, the Pacific Northwest has only one circuit (the Ninth), which is completely within the region's boundary. The data in table 5.6 are thus limited to a comparison among circuits that lie wholly within a given region.

In the 1925–36 and 1937–45 periods, the variation among circuits within the same region is small compared to interregional variation. (The negative results are not displayed.) In contrast, the data in table 5.6 suggest that in the postwar periods, circuit variation within regions is common. For

TABLE 5.6. Circuit-Level Differences in Liberal Voting within Regions (by issue area and time period, in percentages)

Region	Circuit	1946–60	1961–69	1970–88
Civil rights and liberties				
Northeast	1st	23	20	29
	2d	16	24	31
	3d	36	23	37
	Circuit difference	20	4	8
South	4th	12	33	27
	5th	29	19	30
	11th	—	—	32
	Circuit difference	17	14	5
Great Plains/Rocky Mountains	7th	25	20	31
	10th	24	18	29
	Circuit difference	1	2	2
	Regional difference	14	10	6
Criminal				
Northeast	1st	23	18	22
	2d	14	21	27
	3d	36	18	26
	Circuit difference	22	3	5
South	4th	11	30	21
	5th	27	17	25
	11th	—	—	—
	Circuit difference	16	13	4
Great Plains/Rocky Mountains	7th	18	19	22
	10th	20	18	21
	Circuit difference	2	1	1
	Regional difference	12	8	6
Labor and economic regulation				
Northeast	1st	60	48	57
	2d	39	56	52
	3d	49	51	57
	Circuit difference	21	8	5
South	4th	56	42	50
	5th	46	63	46
	11th	—	—	67
	Circuit difference	10	21	21
Great Plains/Rocky Mountains	7th	55	52	51
	10th	54	54	60
	Circuit difference	1	2	9
	Regional difference	13	11	2

civil rights and liberties cases, in all three postwar time periods, at least one region has greater variation in outcomes among its constituent circuits than the range of differences among the four regions. For example, in the 1946–60 time period, the 17-percentage-point differential between the proportion of liberal votes in the Fourth and Fifth Circuits of the South (29 vs. 12 percent) is greater than the range of 14 percent between the most liberal and most conservative regions.[6] In the Northeast region, intercircuit variation was 20 percent, a figure considerably higher than the average interregion variation.

A similar pattern exists for labor and economic cases. In all three time periods (1946–60, 1961–69, and 1970–88), the variation between circuits within at least one of the regions is greater than the average differences among regions. The results are especially striking for the 1970–88 period. The regional analysis presented above showed virtually no regional variation. However, within the South, substantial variation existed among circuits, from a high of 67 percent liberal in the Eleventh Circuit to a low of 46 percent in the Fifth Circuit. While the differences are not quite as extreme for criminal cases, the overall pattern is not markedly different. For both the 1946–60 and 1961–69 time periods, the variation among southern circuits is greater than the average differences among regions, and for the 1946–60 period, the variation among circuits in the Northeast also exceeds the range of differences among the four regions. In sum, while important regional variation exists, it appears that intercircuit differences account for a greater portion of variation in judicial decision making.

Conclusion

This analysis of patterns in decision making on the courts of appeals revealed substantial continuity and change over time and across circuits. Several general trends in decision making that had not been identified in previous studies of decision making for shorter time periods are noteworthy. First, the courts have become decidedly more conflictual since the New Deal. Currently, the rate of dissent is roughly three times as high as it was in the 1920s. This increasing conflict on the courts is likely due to a number of factors including changes in Supreme Court behavior, movement over time toward more ideologically oriented appointment criteria (see chap. 2), the changing agenda of the courts (see chap. 3), and an increasing tendency toward nonpublication of many of the more routine decisions of the courts. Still, as the rate of dissent generally increased over time, wide variation characterized the different circuits. In every time period, cases in some circuits were more than twice as likely to be decided non-unanimously than cases in other circuits at the same time. Further investigation will be required to untangle the reasons for these intercircuit differences. As a starting point for those investigations, it might be noted that earlier work has uncovered substantial differences among circuits in both their issue agendas and norms regarding publication (Howard 1981; Songer 1991). Since both of these factors appear to be related to overall rates of dissent, the variation in the incidence of these factors may account for some or most of the intercircuit differences.

A second significant finding has been that the partisan basis of voting in the courts of appeals that has been widely documented in previous studies appears to be only a postwar phenomenon. Since empirical analyses of the courts of appeals are relatively recent and few (compared to studies of the High Court), the near absence of party differences in judicial voting from 1925 to 1945 revealed in our analysis had not been previously recognized. Nevertheless, our finding that partisan-based voting trends have been with us for a half century, coupled with our finding (chap. 2) that even within single time periods there are often substantial circuit differences in the partisan makeup of the bench, suggests the potential for variation in circuit law and policy as a result of the uneven patterns of judicial replacement across circuits. We hope that the discovery that the extent of partisan polarization varies over time will stimulate new research into the conditions that produce or encourage partisan division on the courts.

While partisan effects have increased over time, regional differences have declined. In fact, in all three issue areas examined, regional disparities in the 1970s and 1980s have shrunk to less than one-fourth of the magnitude of those differences in the 1920s and 1930s. In labor and economic cases the difference between the most liberal and most conservative region has nearly vanished, shrinking to a mere 2.4 percent in the period since 1970. The most dramatic declines were evident in criminal cases, where regional differences of nearly 30 percent in the 1925–36 period have steadily shrunk over time before falling to 6.4 percent in the 1970–88 period. These results have important implications for much of the research on courts that has utilized some measure of regionalism in models of judicial voting. Relatedly, our analysis also supports the findings of existing studies that suggest circuits are not good proxies for regions in the study of judicial behavior on the lower courts. Substantial intercircuit differences in judicial voting emerged within regions. These results argue for studying circuits from an institutional perspective that recognizes the importance of formal rules and informal norms in shaping judicial choice.

When these trends are considered together, the overall picture that emerges suggests that the politics of the courts of appeals are increasingly becoming nationalized. At a time when the level of overt conflict is increasing in the judiciary, the battle lines are increasingly drawn along the lines of national party differences. The efforts of recent administrations to advance policy goals through judicial selection have likely enhanced party-based differences on the appeals courts. To the extent that decentralized forces influence judicial behavior, our findings indicate that circuit boundaries offer more promise for future research as the explanatory power of regional perspectives has diminished.

CHAPTER 6

Conclusion: Continuity and Change in the U.S. Courts of Appeals

The period of our analysis, 1925 through 1988, allowed us to observe the U.S. Courts of Appeals during a period of maturation in which the courts evolved from a relatively obscure institution predominantly concerned with error correction in private law contests, to one in which the circuits frequently stand at the center of policy-making in public law disputes. The longitudinal perspective adopted for this analysis suggested that several changes in these courts could be attributed to many factors—including social, institutional, legal, and political forces. However, these forces also appeared to contribute to some streams of continuity in the U.S. Courts of Appeals.

The U.S. Courts of Appeals in the Judicial Hierarchy

At the start of the twentieth century, the U.S. Courts of Appeals consisted of a collection of middle-tier tribunals designed to serve a screening function on behalf of the Supreme Court, thereby eliminating the increasing demands on the High Court's docket. Implicit in this role was the acceptance that the appeals courts would perform primarily functions associated with error correction while the Supreme Court would remain the leader in declarations of legal policy. In subsequent years, Congress continued to pass legislation giving the Supreme Court even greater control over its docket. During the same time period, a range of social, institutional, legal, and political forces fueled appellate litigation in the federal judiciary. The rising caseloads of the U.S. Courts of Appeals, recently estimated at over 37,000 cases per year, coupled with the lack of review by the Supreme Court, has contributed to greater autonomy for the appeals courts. As noted by former Supreme Court Justice Byron White:

The Supreme Court of the United States reviews only a small percentage of all judgments issued by the twelve courts of appeals. Each of the courts of appeals, therefore, is for all practical purposes the final expositor of the federal law within its geographical jurisdiction. This crucial fact makes each of those courts a tremendously important influence in the development of the federal law, both constitutional and statutory. (Byron R. White, Dedication—Fifth Circuit Symposium, 15 *Texas Tech Law Review* (1984))

As Justice White's comments indicate, the U.S. Courts of Appeals now represent the last stop for most litigants and, not surprisingly, stand at the forefront in the development of several areas of legal policy. As the numbers of litigants and cases have risen over time in the federal courts, judges on the courts of appeals have been forced to address a wider range of issues before their courts. Across the period of our analysis, the agenda of the appeals courts has undergone several changes. In earlier periods, private economic disputes, such as those focusing on patents, tax, debt collection, and private property consumed a large share of the docket and had a negligible impact beyond the litigants involved in the cases. Although the raw number of private economic appeals has risen substantially over this century, judicial attention has increasingly turned to issues in the realm of public law. More specifically, we found that individual litigants have turned to the appeals courts in increasing numbers over the years, and, in many instances, their claims have raised civil rights and liberties issues. Moreover, judicial business has increasingly focused on economic issues that have policy implications for individuals, groups, organizations, and governments in the political system. For example, we found a substantial increase in attention to broad economic policy questions involving governmental regulation and labor relations. These changes in the docket of the appeals courts have contributed to their role as a policy-making institution as judges have shifted their focus from private commercial matters to questions associated with civil liberties, civil rights, and governmental economic issues.

In addition to fueling changes in the issue agenda, higher caseloads in the appeals courts have highlighted the constraints associated with the ability of the Supreme Court to provide oversight in the judicial hierarchy. In the early years of our analysis, the Supreme Court was reviewing around 5 percent of appeals court cases, whereas in recent years the Court reviewed less than one-fourth of 1 percent. The sheer numbers of cases heard by the appeals courts makes it impossible for the Supreme Court to adequately monitor the lower courts. In 1984 Justice Rehnquist stated this explicitly:

> The Court cannot review a sufficiently significant portion of the decisions of the federal court of appeals to maintain the supervisory authority that it maintained over the federal courts fifty years ago; it simply is not able or willing, given the other constraints upon its time, to review all the decisions that result in a conflict in the applicability of federal law. (Rehnquist 1984, 4–5)

Justice Rehnquist's acknowledgment of the changing role of the appeals courts is consistent with the trends we have identified throughout this book. We found the significant growth in the caseloads of the appeals courts was accompanied by an expanding issue agenda. In addition, over time, decision making on the lower federal courts was increasingly characterized by conflict. The absence of Supreme Court supervision for most appeals court cases has resulted in an increased need for the courts to assume the role of declaring law and concomitantly making policy with their decisions. As a result of the high caseloads and diverse issues before them, the modern-day appeals courts perform both error correction and policy-making functions within the judicial hierarchy.

Continuity in the Courts of Appeals

Our analysis of the appeals courts encompassed a sixty-four-year period in which the institution underwent structural changes resulting in the addition of two circuits and an increase in the number of seats on the bench. We noted above the policy-making effects associated with caseload pressures. The social, political, legal, and institutional environments in which the courts were adjudicating were changing dramatically. Nevertheless, with all of this change, there has remained continuity in some very important aspects of the institution.

Role of Error Correction

In the federal court system in the United States, appeals courts cannot take a "fresh" view of the facts; instead, legal norms and tradition require that appeals concentrate on alleged error(s) made by the trial judge. As a result, appeals court judges view the facts and issues involved in the case from the perspective of the trial judge. In general, issues raised on appeal must have been preserved in the proceedings before the court or administrative agency below. In the course of review, appeals court judges may find trial court judges make errors, but unless the error could have changed the outcome of the case, they will still affirm the judgment below. As originally conceived, the courts of appeals were intended to focus on this role of error correction. Overall, our analysis found judges on the appeals courts tend to adhere to these legal norms in fulfilling this role. Affirming the decision of the judge below was commonplace: across the period of our analysis, reversal rates varied only from 26 to 31 percent, indicating that the appeals courts have been, and continued to be, involved in legitimating lower court rulings.

The low reversal rates should not be surprising, even as the volume of cases varied over time, increasing from 2,525 in 1925 to 37,524 in 1988. While this tremendous increase in judicial business has provided a greater opportunity for the appeals courts to engage in policy-making, the vast majority of appeals fall into the category of ordinary litigation. We estimated that the number of private economic disputes that were decided annually with a published opinion was approximately 1,300 from 1970 through 1988. Moreover, the appeals courts have been inundated with prisoner petitions since the 1960s. In the majority of these routine appeals, the court's decision has little impact beyond the interests of the litigants.

The courts of appeals have met the demands of increasing caseloads and fulfilled their role of error correction by devising shortcuts for handling cases that are "ritualistic" or do not have broad legal policy consequences. Routine appeals do not always require full consideration with a subsequent published opinion but can be summarily decided with a brief statement of the decision. Judges can utilize law clerks in the processing of these cases and, in some circuits, staff attorneys, who will examine the arguments and draft a recommendation that may form the basis of the court's decision. In recent years, appeals court judges have relied increasingly on the use of brief unpublished opinions. Even in cases where appeals court judges find reversible error, they may decide to remand a case for further proceedings in the court below. With the number of appeals continuing to increase and the number of seats on the bench remaining relatively constant, it is inevitable that the use of these and other mechanisms for efficiently moving cases through the appeals courts will continue to grow.

Haves versus Have-Nots

The threat of angry litigants that "I will take my case all the way to the Supreme Court" is well known, but those who study the courts realize it is also inaccurate. A more accurate rendition for litigants in federal courts would be "I will take my case all the way to the courts of appeals." The appeals courts are the final arbiter for virtually all litigants in the federal system with the Supreme Court reviewing less than 1 percent of their cases. The litigation explosion increased the responsibility of the appeals courts as final arbiter, but it also brought about changes in the nature of litigants appearing before the courts. In the early years of our analysis, the appeals courts served as a forum primarily for business litigants; however, in the periods following World War II, particularly in the years following the 1960s, we have seen a dramatic increase in the percentage of cases involving individuals. The increased participation by individuals is a result of many factors, including actions by Congress and the Supreme Court that facilitated individual access to the federal courts. For example, the passage of civil rights statutes created a cause of action for individuals seeking legal redress for alleged discrimination in employ-ment, housing, and transportation. The reinterpretation of existing statutes by the Supreme Court also encouraged litigation in civil rights. Additional landmark decisions of the High Court broadening the scope of the Bill of Rights, particularly in the area of criminal procedure, likely encouraged individuals, including criminal defendants, to pursue their appeal. Recognizing the need to make justice accessible, Supreme Court decisions and statutes enacted by Congress substantially reduced the costs of appeal initiated by criminal defendants and prisoners. In the broader social environment, increased awareness of individual rights and liberties was fueled by social and political movements whose leaders increasingly perceived the federal courts as a viable forum for pursuing policy goals.

While litigants with fewer resources were utilizing the appeals courts in greater numbers across time, their success rates in this forum remained very low. The haves consistently won more often than the have-nots in the courts of appeals. Our analysis of success rates demonstrates that one con-stant in the decisional history of the appeals court is that parties with fewer resources are less likely to succeed. Individuals lost over 60 percent of their cases, businesses won less than 50 percent, and governments won a major-ity of their cases during the 1925–88 period. This finding is consistent with a substantial body of literature suggesting "repeat player haves" are more likely to succeed in litigation because of experience and financial resources.

As highlighted in our analysis in the fourth chapter, success rates of classes of litigants remained stable over a period of time in which there were significant changes that should have favored disadvantaged litigants. We suggested that one possible reason for this finding may be tied to changes in levels of participation over time. As the legal environment changed with landmark decisions by the Supreme Court in the 1960s and, later, with civil rights legislation passed by Congress, individuals increasingly turned to the courts. Although the law was more favorable to meritorious claims, changes in legal doctrine also may have encouraged litigants to appeal unfavorable cases that would not have been pursued in earlier years. As a result, the success rates of individuals may appear to be low even though more individuals were winning, either on appeal or earlier in the litigation process.

Similarly, changes in constitutional law regarding the right to counsel, along with legislation ensuring defendants' legal representation through various stages of federal litigation, also should have helped to offset the advantage of governmental litigants in criminal cases. However, again, the success rates of individuals in criminal appeals were relatively low. Criminal defendants, armed with "free counsel," will push for appeals, regardless of their merit. As these examples illustrate, the courts increasingly became a forum for have-nots; however, higher rates of participation did not translate into increased success in the U.S. Courts of Appeals.

Judicial Selection

Presidents have historically recognized the importance of judicial appointments to the federal bench. Although presidents place greater emphasis on Supreme Court appointments, lower court appointments do not go by unnoticed. The extent to which administrations focus on appeals court appointments has varied over time and for different presidents. Moreover, the strategies followed by different presidents in making appointments has also varied depending on the influence of senatorial courtesy, the presence of divided government, and the salience of judicial appointments in the presidential policy agenda. Some presidents have utilized strategies based on patronage, rewarding allies and political friends. Other presidents, such as Franklin Roosevelt and Ronald Reagan, engaged in a policy-oriented strategy in which appointments were based on the political positions of candidates. Most presidents employ partisan agendas that, at a minimum, ensure the appointment of the party faithful. Not surprisingly, presidential appointments strategies generally have contributed to a bench that is distinctly partisan. This characteristic remained prevalent throughout the period of our analysis. Presidents appoint members of their own party. There were very few cross-party appointments by presidents, even by Republican presidents who were appointing individuals under a divided government.

Our analysis suggested that only a few differences in the strategies utilized by Democratic and Republican presidents resulted in varying appointment cohorts. Since Republicans have generally served during divided government and therefore were not as constrained by senatorial courtesy, they have had more discretion in their appointments. In the earlier years, Republican presidents focused more on judicial qualifications, in contrast to their Democratic counterparts who generally followed a partisan strategy. Democratic presidents have served more often during periods of united government and subsequently faced senatorial courtesy in developing their appointment strategies. As a result, their appointments tended to reflect the interests of home-state senators from the president's party. These partisan differences in the career backgrounds of appeals court nominees were apparent in the earlier years of the appeals courts, but they declined over the time period we studied. While partisan differences in career paths diminished over time, presidents varied in their efforts to bring diversity to the bench in recent years. This push for diversity on the bench during the Carter years contributed to very limited variation in the race, gender, and ethnicity of appointees. In spite of these efforts, the demographic portrait of appeals court judges continued to be very similar to that of their predecessors on the bench: Caucasian, male, and Protestant. Our composite profile suggests that judges on the federal appellate bench tended to be similar in their career paths as well.[1]

Change in the Courts of Appeals

Although there are streams of continuity during the period of our analysis, the appeals courts were not insulated from the environmental changes occurring around them. These changes contributed to an increased policy-making role for the appeals courts. As judges turned more attention to policy-making appeals, their decisions were more likely to reflect cleavages associated with their preferences. Although the structural boundaries of the federal courts would suggest regional variation to characterize these policy differences, our analysis found that, over time, decision-making cleavages shaped by place-based cultural differences were replaced by divisions associated with political party affiliation and the institutional features of the circuits.

Appeals Courts as Policymakers

Earlier in this chapter, we noted that changes in caseloads over time provided judges with more opportunities to make policy in areas of public law. Evidence of this trend may be attributed to changes in the types of issues addressed by these courts. Over time, our analysis documented a shift in judicial business from private law contests to questions requiring the application or interpretation of statutes and the Constitution. Given the low probability of these cases being reviewed by the Supreme Court, the decisions of the appeals court stand as precedent for the circuit. As such, their decisions constrain the actions of other federal judges (within the circuit), the arguments raised by attorneys involved in litigation, and ultimately the behavior of individuals, businesses, and governmental organizations seeking to conform to the "law." The agenda of these courts also evidenced an increase in issues raising civil rights and liberties and public economic questions. Unlike private economic disputes, these appeals require judges to consider the policy-making implications of a decision that will contribute to precedent at the circuit level. Since the appeals courts do not have control over the cases on their docket,[2] the transformation of the issue agenda reflects, in part, the decisions of parties to pursue litigation and, later, to appeal the outcome. This decision may be shaped by a variety of influences, including the perceived receptivity of the circuit to their claim, an assessment of favorable precedent (including decisions of the Supreme Court), and statutory changes by Congress that can create the legal basis for the claim. As a result, unlike the Supreme Court, the U.S. Courts of Appeals' policy-making role is shaped by dynamic forces within and outside of the legal system.

In addition to shifts in the broad categories of case types, the questions before the appeals courts appear to have become more complex over time, suggesting greater involvement in the "details" of policy-making issues. One indicator of increased complexity is the length of the majority opinion. Complex cases require more detailed analysis and explanation in the opinions, whereas routine error-correcting cases are often decided with short brief statements of the decision. In the first period (1925–36), the rate of opinions written in less than one page was approximately 11 percent. In the most recent period (1970–88), the rate of published decisions that were less than one page declined to 2 percent. A comparison of the same time periods found the percentage of decisions with opinions over two pages increased, from 63 to 89 percent. While this is admittedly a very rough measure of case complexity, one could safely argue that short opinions resolve "routine" questions, while longer opinions reflect on the number of issues that the majority on the panel believes must be addressed in the court's decision.

Our analysis also suggested that decision making was increasingly characterized by conflict between judges hearing the appeal. We found a significant increase in the rate of dissent in the courts of appeals across the sixty-four-year period. In the early years, the dissent rate hovered around 3 percent. Since the late 1930s, the rate tripled so that in the most recent period, approximately 9½ percent of the decisions of these courts were non-unanimous. Increasing levels of dissent are one indicator of increased policy-making, since we would expect greater disagreement in cases with policy implications. Moreover, we find that there are differences in rates of dissent across issue areas with civil rights and liberties having the highest rate of dissent. Overall, the results clearly suggest that changes in the issue agenda (with more policy-relevant cases on the docket) were accompanied by higher levels of dissent.

Although the clear majority of cases were decided unanimously throughout the time period, judges appeared to increasingly disagree with one another over policy issues without appearing divisive. Since the late 1940s, the decisional trends outlined in the fifth chapter indicate that judges appointed by Democratic presidents were more likely to support the liberal position than judges appointed by Republican presidents. However, in the years prior to World War II, we found that partisanship was generally unrelated to decision making. The changing influence of political party on decision making would be consistent with our interpretation of the shift in the courts' policy-making role. Partisanship shaped voting patterns during periods in which changes in the issue agenda offered more policy-making opportunities. Overall, party-based differences were strongest in the later years, particularly in civil rights and liberties cases.

While most legal policy-making and error correction focus on federal legal questions, our analysis suggested that diversity of citizenship cases have long been a staple of judicial business in the appeals courts. In these cases, federal judges are called upon to apply the relevant state substantive law. Designed to protect defendants from bias in an out-of-state forum, diversity of citizenship cases have created a substantial burden for judges in the lower federal courts (Posner 1996). Over the last fifty years, state law in torts, commercial relations, and contracts has undergone dramatic change. Throughout this period of reform, federal judges have had to address issues that at times require extensive analysis of current developments in state law. In these situations, the law can be unclear. The policy consequences of this uncertainty may bring federal courts to lead developments in state law. As Judge Posner notes,

> the picture of the federal judge as ventriloquist's dummy is overdrawn. Especially in a period when fewer than half of all federal court of appeals' decisions are published, the published decisions of the courts of appeals in diversity cases tend to be ones in which state law is unclear. In such cases the decision must be based on general principles of common law rather than on slavish adherence to established state precedents. . . . So diversity jurisdiction does create a danger of displacing state common law into federal courts. (1996, 217–18)

Our analysis found a substantial percentage of published decisions are devoted to issues raised in diversity of citizenship cases. A closer examination of these cases clearly indicated that most are not focused on legal issues concerning the federal rules of civil procedure. Why, then, would appeals court judges choose to publish decisions in these cases? Posner's insights suggest legal uncertainty would account for some publication decisions. In these situations, establishing circuit precedent may be helpful for federal judges in the circuit as they address future diversity cases dealing with similar substantive state-law issues. Interestingly, one study found that federal appeals courts prefer to cite their own previous diversity decisions rather than cite state-court decisions (Landes and Posner 1980). Since substantive state-law questions resolved by the circuit courts generally are not subject to review by the Supreme Court, the appeals courts have the potential to be de facto policymakers in state law as well as federal law.

Today, the courts of appeals are still predominantly consumed with performing their role of error correction. However, diversity in the issue agenda has brought with it change in the policy-making role of these courts. This new role manifested itself in higher levels of dissent and partisanship in decision making. If caseloads continue to increase and the likelihood of review by the Supreme Court remains low, one can speculate that policy-making will become more prevalent as the circuit courts continue to develop procedural mechanisms that permit them to concentrate on these "hard" cases.

Decentralized Structure and the Nationalization of Conflict

The courts of appeals are structured along geographical lines so that several circuits fall within traditional regional boundaries. It is this structural characteristic that has led many scholars to suggest regional variation is an important component of any explanation of decision making in the lower federal courts. The U.S. Courts of Appeals collectively are a national institution so that its effectiveness may depend on the extent to which these courts assimilate diverse perspectives into coherent legal policy. This tension between decentralized structure and nationalizing influences has been highlighted in a substantial body of research by lower court scholars (Richardson and Vines 1970; Howard 1981). Together, these analyses of the federal courts offer a conflicting picture. Some scholars have found regional interests paralleled decision making on appeals courts (Howard 1981; Wenner and Dutter 1988). Other analyses emphasized how appeals court judges' role perceptions have led them to resist influences from local political forces (Peltason 1961; Howard 1981). Our analysis suggests that a longitudinal perspective helps to clarify the relative importance of centralizing and decentralizing influences on decision making. We explored the impact of region on decision making across the sixty-four-year period and found that regional variation in decisional trends does exist in the early years. However, over time, regions increasingly failed to account for much of the variation in decision making. The decline in regional variation in civil rights and liberties cases was fourfold and in criminal cases it was even more dramatic. Scholars have long made much of the "southern distinctiveness" of courts from that region, but our analysis indicates that this characteristic has all but disappeared. The south was not consistently the most conservative region across issue areas and time periods, even when we control for political party effects in a multivariate analysis.

While regionalism has declined, partisan voting has become increasingly prevalent in the courts of appeals. Since the 1940s, Democratic appointees generally have been more likely to cast a liberal vote than their Republican counterparts. The decline in regional variation and the rise of differences associated with party affiliation suggests that decisional conflicts in the courts of appeals are now rooted in national party–based ideological differences. Increased partisanship in voting parallels the changing appointment strategies of recent presidents with greater emphasis on the role of the president in selecting nominees. The recruitment of those with strong ties to the president and his party contributes to a characterization of the courts in which policy-making would be expected to reflect the political agenda of the national parties rather than local concerns. Appointments based on these criteria led to greater homogeneity among the judges from the same party and resulted in voting patterns that reflect an ideological consensus along national party lines. Moreover, the increased role of the president in selection has meant a decline in home-state senatorial influence in the process, which, in turn, may have contributed to the decline in the influence of regional values. Appeals court judges today are more likely to have been involved in national politics, directly or indirectly, than in earlier periods when politics was much more localized for the majority of the country.

Although regional differences have declined in the appeals courts, our analysis suggests decentralizing influences continue to shape judicial choice. However, it appears to be the institutional features of the circuits that appear to account for place-based variation. To those who argue and appear before the appeals courts, these findings would not be suprising. As described by Judge Posner, the "thirteen courts of appeals constitute at best a loose confederacy" (1996, 380). While appeals court judges may be persuaded by precedent of the other circuits, judges are bound only by the precedent created within the circuit (and from "above"). Circuit conflict clearly exists and plays an important role in determining which issues will be addressed by the High Court. Earlier studies of appeals courts also documented intercircuit differences existing in decision making, but attributed these differences largely to the regional characteristics of the geographical areas circumscribed by circuit borders (Howard 1981). In contrast, our analysis of circuit variation in decision making suggested greater variation among circuits within regions than between circuits from different regions. Moreover, in issue areas where we found virtually no variation among regions in a particular time period, we found substantial variation among circuits during the same time period. The reasons for these differences are far from clear, but insights from an institutional perspective may account for this phenomenon. Such a perspective would suggest that the circuits' varying geographical areas, docket composition, and membership size contribute to differences in circuit legal policy, particularly in the initial stages of a litigation cycle for an area of the law. Decision-making rules and informal norms can help to sharpen these differences between the circuits as subsequent litigation in a specific area of the law further refines policy-making issues. We recognize that our ideas here are speculative, since additional research is needed to explore the reasons for cohesion within a circuit, as well as intercircuit conflict.

Another factor accounting for the nationalization of conflict can be attributed to changes in the role of the federal government in American society over the sixty-four-year period of our analysis. Beginning in the 1930s, the federal government began to take an active role in the regulation of the economy, a role that has only increased during the subsequent decades. The New Deal introduced the era of federal regulation. Although administrative agencies are guided by legislative mandates, statutes tend to be vague, delegating substantial powers to administrators. As agencies have grown in terms of their impact on public policy, judicial oversight has increased as well. Our analysis indicated that in the last fifty years the courts of appeals found itself increasingly involved in hearing appeals in which one of the parties was an administrative agency. Many of these appeals require judges to engage in statutory interpretation, a process that requires ascertaining the underlying purpose of a statute and legislative intent. These canons of interpretation would lead judges to define legal policy in terms that relate to national concerns.

It is evident that the courts of appeals have evolved into an institution that addresses a wide variety of issues often involving the application or interpretation of legal principles derived from federal statutes or the Constitution. Their increased policy-making role, coupled with limited review by the High Court, has led presidents to focus more attention on the selection of appeals court judges. The politicization of judicial selection has given rise to increased partisanship in the voting of judges and brought about what would seem to be a nationalization of conflict. Although the courts of appeals may have originally been conceived as regional appellate courts, they have evolved into a modern-day institution staffed by men and women whose decisions are frequently shaped by policy views that mirror the beliefs of the president responsible for their appointment.

Conclusion

The courts of appeals were originally created to alleviate the docket pressures being placed on the Supreme Court in the late nineteenth century. It was the intent of Congress that these intermediate appeals courts would perform the function of error correction, leaving declarations of law to the Supreme Court. The explosion in litigation during the twentieth century brought about a second docket crisis; however, this crisis centered on the caseloads of the appeals courts. Absent the creation of another layer of the judiciary, the appeals courts increasingly found themselves performing the policy-making role originally intended for the High Court. Even so, the appeals courts are still primarily involved in correcting errors from below. The twentieth century was a period consisting of both change and continuity for the courts of appeals. As they adapted to changes in the social, political, and legal environments, the modern-day appeals courts appear very different along some dimensions than they did sixty years ago, but along other dimensions they are the same.

Appendix: Description of the U.S. Courts of Appeals Data Base

A Multiuser Data Base Created by a Grant from the National Science Foundation (SES-8912678)

Principal Investigator:
Donald R. Songer
Professor of Political Science
University of South Carolina
Columbia, SC 29208
e-mail: Dsonger@sc.edu

The data are archived at the ICPSR in three forms: an SPSS file, an SAS file, and an ASCII file (i.e., raw data). Users should select the format that will be easiest for them to utilize. In the variable list below, the acronym listed after the variable number represents the variable name as it appears in both the SPSS and SAS versions of the data. The ASCII file is provided in a fixed column, rectangular format with a logical record length of 609. The size of the data base in its ASCII version is slightly over ten megabytes. A file containing the detailed documentation of the data is available in a Word Perfect format.

Each of the files in the appeals court data base is also available from the web page of the Program for Law and Judicial Politics of Michigan State University. Both data files and the documentation can be downloaded directly from the web page. The address of the web page is:

http://www.ssc.msu.edu/~pls/pljp

Variable List

The variable list that follows is organized by topical categories of variables. The description of variables that follows proceeds in the same order. The acronym associated with each variable is the variable name contained in both the SAS and SPSS versions of the data base.

Basic Case Characteristics

A. General Description

1. CASENUM   case identification
2. YEAR   year of decision
3. MONTH   month of decision
4. DAY   day of decision
5. CITE   citation in *Federal Reporter*
6. VOL   volume in which case located
7. BEGINPG   page number of first page of case
8. ENDOPIN   page number of last page of majority opinion
9. ENDPAGE   page number of last page of all opinions in case
10. DOCNUM   docket number of first case decided by the opinion
11. METHOD   nature of appeals court decision (e.g., first decision by
                three-judge panel, *en banc*)

B. History and Nature of Case

12. CIRCUIT   circuit of court
13. STATE   state of origin of case
14. DISTRICT   district of origin of case
15. ORIGIN   type of court or agency that made original decision
16. SOURCE   forum from which decision appealed
17. DISTJUDG   identity of district judge (if any) deciding case below
18. APPLFROM   type of district court final judgment (if any) appealed
                from
19. ADMINREV   identity of federal regulatory agency (if any) the case
                was appealed from
20. PRIORPUB   citation (if any) to prior published opinion in district
                court
21. OPINSTAT   opinion status of decision
22. CLASSACT   was case a class action?
23. CROSSAPP   were there cross appeals?
24. SANCTION   were sanctions imposed?
25. INITIATE   party initiating appeal (e.g., plaintiff, defendant,
                intervenor)

Participants

A. Appellants

26. NUMAPPEL	total number of appellants
27. APPNATPR	number of appellants who were natural persons
28. APPBUS	number of appellants who were private businesses
29. APPNONP	number of appellants who were nonprofit groups
30. APPFED	number of appellants who were federal government agencies
31. APPSUBST	number of appellants who were substate governments
32. APPSTATE	number of appellants who were state government agencies
33. APPFIDUC	number of appellants who were fiduciaries or trustees
34. APP_STID	state of appellant (if appellant is state or local govt)
35. GENAPEL1	general classification of first appellant
36. BANK_AP1	was first appellant bankrupt?
37. APPEL1	detailed nature of first listed appellant
38. GENAPEL2	general classification of second appellant
39. BANK_AP2	was second appellant bankrupt?
40. APPEL2	detailed nature of second listed appellant whose code is not identical to the code of the first appellant
41. REALAPP	are the appellants coded in var 37 and var 40 the real parties in this case

B. Respondents

42. NUMRESP	total number of respondents
43. R_NATPR	number of respondents who were natural persons
44. R_BUS	number of respondents who were private businesses
45. R_NONP	number of respondents who were nonprofit groups
46. R_FED	number of respondents who were federal government agencies
47. R_SUBST	number of respondents who were substate governments
48. R_STATE	number of respondents who were state government agencies
49. R_FIDUC	number of respondents who were fiduciaries or trustees

50. R_STID	state of respondent (if respondent is state or local govt)
51. GENRESP1	general classification of first respondent
52. BANK_R1	was first respondent bankrupt?
53. RESPOND1	detailed nature of first listed respondent
54. GENRESP2	general classification of second respondent
55. BANK_R2	was second respondent bankrupt?
56. RESPOND2	detailed nature of second listed respondent whose code is not identical to the code of the first respondent
57. REALRESP	are the respondents coded in field 53 and field 56 the real parties in this case?

C. Other Participants

58. COUNSEL1	counsel for appellant
59. COUNSEL2	counsel for respondent
60. AMICUS	number of amicus curiae briefs filed
61. INTERVEN	was there an intervenor?

Issues Coding

A. Basic Nature of Issue and Decision

62. CASETYP1	first case type—substantive policy (analogous to Spaeth issue codes)
63. GENISS	eight summary issue categories based on CASETYP1
64. DIRECT1	directionality of decision on first case type
65. CASETYP2	second case type
66. DIRECT2	directionality of decision on second case type
67. TREAT	treatment of decision below by appeals court
68. MAJVOTES	number of majority votes
69. DISSENT	number of dissenting votes
70. CONCUR	number of concurrences
71. HABEAS	was this a habeas corpus case?
72. DECUNCON	was law or administrative action declared unconstitutional?
73. CONSTIT	was there an issue about the constitutionality of a law or administrative action?
74. FEDLAW	did the court engage in statutory interpretation?
75. PROCEDUR	was there an interpretation of precedent that did not involve statutory or constitutional interpretation?

| 76. TYPEISS | general nature of proceedings (criminal, civil-government, civil-private, diversity) |

B. Most Frequently Cited Constitutional Provisions, Statutes, and Procedural Rules

77. CONST1	constitutional provision most frequently cited in headnotes
78. CONST2	constitutional provision second most frequently cited in headnotes
79. USC1	title of US Code most frequently cited in headnotes
80. USC1SECT	section of USC1 most frequently cited in headnotes
81. USC2	title of US Code second most frequently cited in headnotes
82. USC2SECT	section of USC2 most frequently cited in headnotes
83. CIVPROC1	Federal Rule of Civil Procedure most frequently cited in headnotes
84. CIVPROC2	Federal Rule of Civil Procedure second most frequently cited in headnotes
85. CRMPROC1	Federal Rule of Criminal Procedure most frequently cited in headnotes
86. CRMPROC2	Federal Rule of Criminal Procedure second most frequently cited in headnotes

C. Threshold issues

87. JURIS	was there a jurisdiction issue?
88. STATECL	was there an issue about failure to state a claim?
89. STANDING	was there an issue about standing?
90. MOOTNESS	was there an issue about mootness?
91. EXHAUST	was there an issue about ripeness or failure to exhaust administrative remedies?
92. TIMELY	was there an issue about whether litigants complied with a rule about timeliness, filing fees, or statutes of limitation?
93. IMMUNITY	was there an issue about governmental immunity?
94. FRIVOL	was there an issue about whether the case was frivolous?
95. POLQUEST	was there an issue about the political question doctrine?
96. OTHTHRES	was there some other threshold issue at the trial level?
97. LATE	was there an issue relating to the timeliness of the appeal?
98. FRIVAPP	was there an allegation that the appeal was frivolous?

99. OTHAPPTH   was there some other threshold issue at the appellate
                  level?

D. Criminal issues (for each of the issues below, the coding
captures whether the issue was discussed in the opinion and if so
whether the resolution of the issue favored the appellant or the
respondent)

100. PREJUD   prejudicial conduct by prosecutor
101. INSANE   insanity defense
102. IMPROPER   improper influence on jury
103. JURYINST   jury instructions
104. OTHJURY   other issues relating to juries
105. DEATHPEN   death penalty
106. SENTENCE   issue relating to sentence other than death penalty
107. INDICT   was indictment defective
108. CONFESS   admissibility of confession or incriminating statement
109. SEARCH   admissibility of evidence from search or seizure
110. OTHADMIS   admissibility of evidence other than search or confession
111. PLEA   issue relating to plea bargaining
112. COUNSEL   ineffective counsel
113. RTCOUNS   right to counsel
114. SUFFIC   sufficiency of evidence
115. INDIGENT   violation of rights of indigent
116. ENTRAP   entrapment
117. PROCDIS   dismissal by district court on procedural grounds
118. OTHCRIM   other criminal issue

E. Civil Law Issues

119. DUEPROC   due process
120. EXECORD   interpretation of executive order or administrative
                   regulation
121. STPOLICY   interpretation of state or local law, executive order or
                   administrative regulation
122. WEIGHTEV   interpretation of weight of evidence issues
123. PRETRIAL   trial court rulings on pretrial procedure (but not motions
                   for summary judgment or discovery which are covered in
                   separate variables—see fields 130 and 135)
124. TRIALPRO   court rulings on trial procedure
125. POST_TRL   posttrial procedures and motions (including court costs
                   and motions to set aside jury decisions)
126. ATTYFEE   attorney's fees

127. JUDGDISC	abuse of discretion by trial judge
128. ALTDISP	issue relating to alternative dispute resolution process (includes ADR, settlement conference, mediation, arbitration)
129. INJUNCT	validity or appropriateness of injunction
130. SUMMARY	summary judgment
131. FEDVST	conflict of laws or dispute over whether federal versus state law governs
132. FOREIGN	conflict over whether foreign or domestic law applies
133. INT_LAW	application of international law
134. ST_V_ST	conflict over which state's laws apply
135. DISCOVER	conflict over discovery procedures
136. OTHCIVIL	other civil law issue

F. Civil Law Issues Involving Government Actors,
Administrative Law

137. SUBEVID	substantial evidence doctrine
138. DENOVO	use of standard of review, "de novo on facts"
139. ERRON	clearly erroneous standard
140. CAPRIC	arbitrary or capricious standard
141. ABUSEDIS	should court defer to agency discretion?
142. JUDREV	conflict over whether agency decision was subject to judicial review?
143. GENSTAND	did agency articulate the appropriate general standard?
144. NOTICE	did agency give proper notice?
145. ALJ	did court support decision of administrative law judge?
146. AGEN_ACQ	issue related to agency acquisition of information
147. FREEINFO	administrative denial of information to those requesting it, freedom of information, sunshine laws
148. COMMENT	did agency give proper opportunity to comment?
149. RECORD	did agency fail to develop an adequate record?

G. Diversity Issues

| 150. DIVERSE | were the parties truly diverse? |
| 151. WHLAWS | which state's laws should govern dispute? |

Judges and Votes

160. CODEJ1	code for the judge who wrote the court opinion
161. CODEJ2	code for second judge on panel
162. J2VOTE1	vote of second judge on first case type

163. J2VOTE2	vote of second judge on second case type
164. J2MAJ1	was second judge in majority on first case type?
165. J2MAJ2	was second judge in majority on second case type?
166. CODEJ3	code for third judge on panel
167. J3VOTE1	vote of third judge on first case type
168. J3VOTE2	vote of third judge on second case type
169. J3MAJ1	was third judge in majority on first case type?
170. J3MAJ2	was third judge in majority on second case type?
171. CODEJ4	code for fourth judge on panel
172. J4VOTE1	vote of fourth judge on first case type
173. J4VOTE2	vote of fourth judge on second case type
174. J4MAJ1	was fourth judge in majority on first case type?
175. J4MAJ2	was fourth judge in majority on second case type?
176. CODEJ5	code for fifth judge on panel
177. J5VOTE1	vote of fifth judge on first case type
178. J5VOTE2	vote of fifth judge on second case type
179. J5MAJ1	was fifth judge in majority on first case type?
180. J5MAJ2	was fifth judge in majority on second case type?

.

.

.

225. CODEJ15	code for fifteenth judge on panel
226. J15VOTE1	vote of fifteenth judge on first case type
227. J15VOTE2	vote of fifteenth judge on second case type
228. J15MAJ1	was fifteenth judge in majority on first case type?
229. J15MAJ2	was fifteenth judge in majority on second case type?

Notes

Chapter 1

1. For criticism of the Sears decision, see, for example, 140 F.3d. 288, *McMillan v. Massachusetts Society for the Prevention of Cruelty to Animals* (1st Cir. 1998), 885 F.2d. 575, *EEOC v. GenTel Co. of Northwest* (9th Cir. 1989); and 975 F.2d. 1518, *Miranda v. B&B Cash Grocery Store* (11th Cir. 1992).

2. See, for example, Williams 1989; Eichner 1988; Frug 1992.

3. WESTLAW search indicates that Judge Hand has been quoted in 199 opinions authored by Supreme Court justices.

4. J. Stevens's concurring opinion in *Connecticut National Bank v. Germain*, 503 U.S. 249, 255, quotes from *Lehigh Valley Coal Co. v. Yensavage*, 218 F.547 (2d Cir., 1914).

5. U.S. Constitution, art. 3, sec. 1.

6. Thus, although there were three types of courts, there were only two different types of judges. All of the judges serving on the circuit courts had additional duties sitting on either the Supreme Court or the district courts.

7. This view was particularly strong among justices of the Supreme Court who had to "ride circuit," traveling as much as 1,000 miles twice a year to sit on the circuit court sessions in each of the states covered by "their" circuit.

8. While in 1797 there were thirteen districts, each consisting of a single, whole state, in later years some states were divided into several districts—but no district included territory from more than one state.

9. Each state has from one to four judicial districts within its borders, with the number of districts within a state *roughly* reflecting its population.

10. The number of judges appointed to each district is roughly proportional to the size of the district's caseload, but also appears to reflect the political power of the state's congressional delegation at the time of the last bill to increase the total number of federal judges.

11. These cases are primarily disputes between the governments of two or more states and civil suits against ambassadors.

12. Knibb notes that the first step in determining whether judicial review will originate in the district court or the courts of appeals requires an examination of the statutory text. He also notes that if it is unclear, the circuit court will determine which court has jurisdiction; however, as a general rule, unless Congress gave a firm indication in the statute that it should be in district court, judicial review will originate in the circuit court (1997, 306).

13. For example, it may be rational for an indigent convicted felon to appeal even if his chances of winning are small because he will have all of his legal fees paid for by the government. Therefore, the expected utility of an appeal will be positive even if the probability of winning is small. Alternatively, an insurance company, with in-house counsel who draws a set salary, can postpone paying a large judgment entered by the trial court until all appeals are exhausted by appealing. If their legal expenses are relatively fixed whether they appeal or not it may make economic sense to appeal even with a low chance of victory.

14. The authors' favorite example of such an "easy" case is *Windsor v. Pan American Airways*, 744 F.2d. 1187 (1984). Windsor brought suit against the airline seeking damages in the amount of four hundred trillion dollars "on the grounds of grand theft . . . with the intent to commit nuclear sabotage." Windsor alleged that Pan American conspired with the family of President Kennedy along with President Carter and former presidents Ford and Reagan. The complaint also demanded the arrest of the widow of Dr. Martin Luther King because she posed a threat to the Roman Catholic Church and its episcopacy. Specifically, Windsor alleged that Mrs. King planned to take over an order of black nuns as a prelude to "install herself as a self-declared 'Black Popess.' " The court of appeals presumably had little trouble reaching a decision to unanimously affirm the district court's dismissal of the suit as "patently frivolous."

15. On fairly rare occasions, only two judges will be assigned to sit on a panel. Panels may sometimes end up with only two members to decide an appeal when one of the members voluntarily recuses himself or herself because of a conflict of interest or when one of the original members dies or becomes ill before the decision has been reached.

16. This figure is an estimate derived from data in the U.S. Courts of Appeals Multi-User Database.

17. The chief judge of the circuit is often the judge who is under seventy years of age and has the most years of service on the court of appeals for the given circuit.

18. After surviving the fierce competition for the coveted positions, the clerks often work for one or two years for an appeals court judge before moving into their own practice.

19. Most law clerks are recent honors graduates of the elite law schools in the country. They are selected by the judge for whom they will work and usually serve one or two years, doing legal research, assisting the judge prepare for oral argument, and writing drafts of court opinions for the judges to consider.

20. The government may not appeal verdicts of not guilty in criminal cases because of the constitutional prohibition relating to double jeopardy.

21. On occasion, the panel of appeals court judges may certify a question to a state court of last resort. In these instances, the panel will request the state's highest court to address a question of law so that the federal circuit court can "correctly" apply the relevant state law to a diversity case.

22. In recent years the Supreme Court has reviewed less than two one-hundredths of one percent of the decisions of federal district court judges.

23. Approximately one of every five published decisions of the courts of appeals involved a decision of some federal agency. Of these appeals involving

agency decisions, 37 percent were reviewed directly by the courts of appeals without any prior district court action. The remaining cases were heard first in district court and then appealed to the courts of appeals. As a general rule (among the most active litigators), most decisions of the Civil Aeronautics Board, the Federal Communications Commission, Federal Energy Regulatory Commission, Federal Power Commission, Federal Maritime Commission, Federal Trade Commission, Interstate Commerce Commission, the National Labor Relations Board, Railroad Retirement Board, and the Securities and Exchange Commission go directly from the government agency to the courts of appeals. In contrast, most decisions of agencies within the cabinet-level departments as well as those from the Equal Employment Opportunity Commission, Immigration and Naturalization Service, the parole boards, the Patent Office, the Postal Service, the Social Security Administration, and the Veterans Administration are examined in the district courts before they reach the courts of appeals.

Chapter 2

1. Senatorial courtesy is an informal practice of the Senate where senators defer to the wishes of a home-state senator who opposes a nominee from that state (Goldman 1997). This norm has forced presidents to work closely with the senators of his party who represent the state in which there is a vacant position. In the district courts, home-state senators wield considerable power over the nomination process. In the U.S. Courts of Appeals, presidents have wider latitude with appointments.

2. The exceptions to this generalization include Presidents Wilson and Roosevelt, both of whom did not ignore partisan considerations (Solomon 1984). Instead, they sought to find a way to appoint someone whose views supported their own in specific policy areas.

3. Another possible contributing factor is that there were relatively few Republicans in the South during the early years of the twentieth century. Republicans who would possess the requisite training and experience to sit on the appeals court bench were likely few in number in the southern circuits.

Chapter 3

1. From July 1, 1988, to June 30, 1989, 40.4 percent of all cases disposed of in the U.S. Courts of Appeals were procedural terminations (Administrative Office of the Courts, Annual Report for 1989).

2. Relatedly, changes in the U.S. Sentencing Guidelines frequently affect the frequency and content of criminal appeals.

3. Section 1 of the KKK Act of 1871 was recodified as 42 USC 1983. Claims brought under this statute are frequently referred to as "Section 1983" cases.

4. This situation was complicated further by the stance taken by the Social Security Administration during the 1980s. Adopting a policy of nonacquiescence, the agency viewed circuit court decisions as binding only for the current case.

5. In this analysis, nonviolent offenses typically included alcohol-related crimes, tax fraud, morals charges, and some white collar crimes (e.g., embezzlement).

6. The chief effort here was an amendment to Title VII, the Pregnancy Discrimination Act, that required employers to treat pregnancy in the same fashion that they treat disabilities.

7. Congress passed the Age Discrimination in Employment Act in 1967 (and amended it in 1974 and 1978) and Rehabilitation Act of 1973. The Americans with Disabilities Act, signed into law in 1990, does not affect our analysis, which ends in 1988.

8. While many leading cases were decided in the 1970s, such as *McDonnell Douglas Corp. v. Green* 411 U.S. 792 (1973), *Griggs v. Duke Power*, 401 U.S. 424 (1971), and *Washington v. Davis* 426 U.S. 229 (1976), a wide range of gray area issues emerged in the circuit courts, ranging from challenges to affirmative action programs to claims where the employer had "mixed motives" (e.g., nondiscriminatory and discriminatory reasons). Questions regarding the burden of proof resulted in the "showdown" between the Supreme Court and Congress over precedent established by *Wards Cove Packing Co. Inc. v. Atonio* 490 U.S. 642 (1989).

9. Similar to our analysis of civil rights decisions, we examine only civil liberties cases decided from 1970 through 1988. The percentage of the docket devoted to these issues in the earlier time periods was relatively small thereby precluding any meaningful breakdown of issue types within this category.

10. The "hard look" doctrine was ultimately adopted by the Supreme Court in *Vermont Yankee Nuclear Power Corp. v. Natural Resources Defense Council, Inc.*, 435 U.S. 519 (1978) but later the Court reversed the DC Circuit in a decision that established a high level of deference to the agency's construction of the relevant statute, *Chevron U.S.A., Inc. v. Natural Resources Defense Council*, 467 U.S. 837 (1984).

11. The exception is the Eleventh Circuit. However, it is difficult to draw comparisons to this circuit as its figures included cases decided from 1982 through 1988. Still, in a separate analysis comparing circuit court attention to civil rights cases in the 1980s, the Eleventh Circuit had a dramatically higher proportion of its docket devoted to these issues when compared to its "sister" circuit—the Fifth Circuit. It is possible that the Eleventh Circuit's issue agenda was related to judicial staffing—most judges on this circuit during the 1980s had been appointed by President Carter.

12. Posner (1996) found that changes in the dollar threshold amount influenced district court filings but the same changes had no effect on appeals court filings.

Chapter 4

1. Diversity cases involve issues of state law, but since the parties reside in different states the federal courts are called on to adjudicate the dispute. The

typical diversity case will have an individual opposing a corporation. For example, in *Rhynes v. Branick Manufacturing Corporation* (629 F.2d 409, 1980), the individual appellant brought suit claiming an injury when a tire exploded inside a safety case. The appellant claimed a defective device that had been manufactured by the respondent. The decision of the appeals court was based on state product liability law rather than federal law.

2. At this time, data containing the same coded information from unpublished decisions over the same time periods are not available in a form that we can analyze. Therefore, we recognize that our results, based solely on published decisions, should be interpreted with some caution.

3. In the process of sampling, we were required to assemble a list of case citations for published decisions of each circuit by year. From this information, we calculated the total number of published decisions of the appeals courts to be 1,932 in 1925; 2,431 in 1937; 1,825 in 1946; 2,864 in 1961; 5,630 in 1970; and 6,301 in 1988. To estimate the number of published decisions in which one of the litigants fell into the business category, we multiplied the total by the estimate for businesses' participation rate for that year (a rate based on sample data).

Chapter 5

1. It is generally recognized that the process of decision making in the U.S. Courts of Appeals differs from that in other appellate courts. Unlike Supreme Court justices, circuit court judges do not have control over their dockets and therefore may exercise less discretion. However, exercising less discretion does not mean that cases do not permit opportunities for policy-making. As we argue here, in many cases, the law is not determinative. Moreover, the rotation of panels within the circuit facilitates the expression of judicial policy preferences without dissent (Atkins 1972).

2. The figures reported in table 5.1 combine decisions in which the courts of appeals either reversed, vacated, reversed and remanded, vacated and remanded, or remanded with instructions the decision below. Partial reversals were counted as reversals.

3. Supreme Court scholars Segal and Cover (1989) have developed exogenous measures of justices' attitudes. They created these measures through content analysis of newspaper editorials about nominees from selected newspapers, written between their time of nomination and confirmation. Unfortunately, comparable data cannot be collected for lower federal court nominees.

4. Tate and Handberg (1991) and Carp and Rowland (1983) are two exceptions. Both studies explicitly examined change over time. While their analyses are helpful, their findings were based on data from the Supreme Court (Tate and Handberg 1991) and the federal trial courts (Carp and Rowland 1983) and, as such, may not be generalizable to the U.S. Courts of Appeals.

5. Haire (1993) employed a multistage analysis to identify regions based on these state-level measures reported by Wright, Erikson, and McIver (1985, 1987, 1989). Utilizing the coordinates from a multidimensional scaling analysis of these data in a cluster analysis, the results initially did not yield geographical contiguous regions, as the Pacific Coast states tended to cluster with the Northeast-Great Lakes states. To smooth out differences caused by these outlying states, additional data indicating the latitude and longitude of state capitals were included in the scaling analysis. The cluster analysis from the coordinates of this two-dimensional solution found regional variation in political behavior in the United States to be accounted for by these four regions.

6. The most liberal region, the South, had 24.7 percent support for the liberal position while the most conservative region, the Great Plains-Rocky Mountain area, had a 10.5 percent liberal ratio, a difference of 14.2 percent.

Chapter 6

1. We recognize that this finding will be time-bound as scholars begin to analyze the backgrounds of federal judges appointed by President Clinton. One recent analysis of Clinton's first-term appointments notes that over half of those appeals court judges appointed during his administration were not Caucasian males (Goldman and Slotnick 1997). Although most studies have not found much evidence to suggest a link between diversity and judicial policy (Songer, Davis, and Haire 1994), this dramatic shift in judicial staffing should lead scholars to re-examine the influence of "nontraditional" judges on the federal courts.

2. Our argument here does not take into account the decision to publish the opinion. While publication decisions permit judges some leeway as they identify more important appeals before them, they cannot formally solicit appeals, nor change the facts of the dispute. Moreover, their function is to focus on legal error. As such, they are generally limited to legal issues that were preserved in the trial court or administrative proceeding.

Court Cases

Apex Oil Co. v. Vanguard Oil and Service Co. 1985. 760 F.2d 417 (2d Cir.).
Barnes v. Oddo. 1954. 219 F.2d (2d Cir.).
Bounds v. Smith. 1977. 430 U.S. 817.
Chevron U.S.A., Inc. v. Natural Resources Defense Council. 1984. 467 U.S. 837.
Connecticut National Bank v. Germain. 503 U.S. 249.
Dressman v. Costle. 1985. 759 F.2d 548 (6th Cir.).
EEOC v. GenTel Co. of Northwest. 1989. 885 F.2d 575. (9th Cir.).
EEOC v. Sears. 1988. 839 F.2d 302 (7th Cir.).
Erie, Lackawanna RR. Co. v. Tompkins. 1938. 304 U.S. 64.
Futrell v. Wyrick. 1983. 716 F.2d 1207 (8th Cir.).
Gideon v. Wainwright. 1963. 372 U.S. 335.
Greater Boston Television Corp. v. FCC. 1970. 444 F.2d 841 (D.C. Cir.).
Griggs v. Duke Power. 1971. 401 U.S. 424.
International Harvester Co. v. Ruckelshaus. 1973. 478 F.2d 615 (D.C. Cir.) (conc. op.).
James Berick and Timothy Culver v. United States. 1983. 710 F.2d 1035. (5th Cir.)
James Earl Buie v. Otis Jones, Sheriff; Frank Armstrong, Chief Jailer; Robert L. Hubbard, Jailer; Cumberland County of North Carolina. 1983. 717 F.2d 925. (4th Cir.).
Lange v. Missouri Pacific Railroad Company. 1983. 703 F.2d 322. (8th Cir).
Lehigh Valley Coal Co. v. Yensavage. 1914. 218 F. 547 (2d Circuit).
Mapp v. Ohio. 1961. 367 U.S. 643.
McDonnell Douglas Corp. v. Green. 1973. 411 U.S. 792.
McMillan v. Massachusetts Society for the Prevention of Cruelty to Animals. 1998. 140 F. 3d. 288 (1st Cir.).
Meritor Savings Bank v. Vinson. 1986. 477 U.S. 57.
Metallizing Engineering Co. v. Kenyon Bearing and Auto Parts Co. 1946. 153 F.2d 516 (2d Cir.).
Miranda v. Arizona. 1966. 384 U.S. 436.
Miranda v. B&B Cash Grocery Store. 1992. 975 F.2d 1518 (11th Cir.).

Para-Chem Southern, Inc v. M. Lowenstein Corporation. 1983. 715 F.2d 128. (4th Cir).

Patterson v. FBI. 1989. 893 F.2d 595. (3rd Cir.).

Pineda-Chinchilla v. United States. 1983. 712 F.2d 942. (5th Cir.).

Rhynes v. Branick Manufacturing Corporation. 1980. 629 F.2d 409. (5th Cir.).

Runnebaum v. Nationsbank. 1997. 123 F.3d 156. (4th Cir.).

Russell Stover Candies v. Federal Trade Commission. 1983. 718 F.2d 256. (8th Cir.).

Strong v. Scharner. 1933. 67 F.2d 687. (6th Cir.).

Tomkins v. Public Service Electric and Gas Co. 1977. 568 F.2d 1044. (3rd Cir.).

United States v. Lowell Brown. 1988. 862 F.2d 1033 (3rd Cir.).

United States v. Abraham Minker. 1954. 217 F.2d 350 (3rd Cir.).

Vermont Yankee Nuclear Power Corp. v. Natural Resources Defense Council, Inc. 1978. 435 U.S. 519.

Wards Cove Packing Co. Inc. v. Atonio. 1989. 490 U.S. 642.

Washington v. Davis. 1976. 426 U.S. 229.

Williams v. Goldsmith. 1983. 701 F.2d 603. (7th Cir.).

Windsor v. Pan American Airways. 1984. 744 F.2d 1187 (5th Cir.).

References

Abramowitz, Howard. 1980. "Is the Revolt Fading? A Note on Party Loyalty among Southern Democratic Congressmen." *Journal of Politics* 42:568–72.

Aldisert, Judge Ruggero J. 1997. "The Role of the Courts in Contemporary Society." In *Judges on Judging*, edited by D. M. O'Brien. Chatham: Chatham House Publishers.

Aldrich, John H., and Forrest Nelson. 1984. *Linear Probability, Logit and Probit Models*. Beverly Hills, CA: Sage.

Atkins, Burton. 1972. "Decision Making Rules and Judicial Strategy on the United States Courts of Appeals." *Western Political Quarterly* 25:626–42.

Baker, Thomas E. 1994. *Rationing Justice on Appeal: The Problems of the U.S. Courts of Appeals*. St. Paul, MN: West Publishing.

Barrow, Deborah J., and Thomas Walker. 1988. *A Court Divided: The Fifth Circuit Courts of Appeals and the Politics of Judicial Reform*. New Haven: Yale University Press.

Barrow, Deborah J., Gary Zuk, and Gerard S. Gryski. 1996. *The Federal Judiciary and Institutional Change*. Ann Arbor: University of Michigan Press.

Baum, Lawrence. 1991. "Specializing the Federal Courts: Neutral Reforms or Efforts to Shape Judicial Policy?" *Judicature* 74:217–24.

Baum, Lawrence, Sheldon Goldman, and Austin Sarat. 1981. "The Evolution of Litigation in the Federal Courts of Appeals." *Law and Society Review* 16:291–309.

Berkson, Larry C., and Susan B. Carbon. 1980. *The United States Circuit Judge Nominating Commission: Its Members, Procedures and Candidates*. Chicago: American Judicature Society.

Brady, David W. 1973. *Congressional Voting in a Partisan Era: A Study of the McKinley Houses and a Comparison to the Modern House of Representatives*. Lawrence: University of Kansas Press.

Campbell, Angus, Philip E. Converse, Warren E. Miller, and Donald E. Stokes. 1960. *The American Voter*. Chicago: University of Chicago Press.

———. 1966. *Elections and the Political Order*. New York: John Wiley and Sons.

Carp, Robert A. 1972. "The Scope and Function of Intra-Circuit Judicial Communications: A Case Study of the Eighth Circuit." *Law and Society Review* 6:405–27.

Carp, Robert A., and C. K. Rowland. 1983. *Policymaking and Politics in the Federal District Courts*. Knoxville: University of Tennessee Press.

Carp, Robert A., and Ronald Stidham. 1991. *The Federal Courts*. 2d ed. Washington, DC: Congressional Quarterly Press.

———. 1998. *The Federal Courts*. 3d ed. Washington, DC: Congressional Quarterly Press.

Carter, Lief H., and Christine B. Harrington. 1991. *Administrative Law and Politics*. New York: Harper Collins.

Chase, Harold. 1972. *Federal Judges: The Appointing Process*. Minneapolis: University of Minnesota Press.

Clausen, Aage R. 1973. *How Congressmen Decide: A Policy Focus*. New York: St. Martin's Press.

Coffin, Frank. 1980. *The Ways of a Judge: Reflections from the Federal Appellate Bench*. Boston: Houghton Mifflin.

———. 1994. *On Appeal: Courts, Lawyering, and Judging*. New York: W. W. Norton.

Conway, M. Margaret, David W. Ahern, and Gertrude A. Steuernagel. 1999. *Women and Public Policy*. Washington, DC: Congressional Quarterly.

Cortner, Richard C. 1968. "Strategies and Tactics of Litigants in Constitutional Cases." *Journal of Public Law* 17:287–307.

Davis, Sue, and Donald R. Songer. 1989. "The Changing Role of the United States Court of Appeals: The Flow of Litigation Revisited." *Justice System Journal* 13:323–30.

Dudley, Robert L. 1989. "Lower Court Decision-Making in Pornography Cases: Do We Know It When We See It?" Paper read at Midwest Political Science Association, at Chicago.

Edwards, Harry T. 1998. "Collegiality and Decision Making on the D.C. Circuit." *Virginia Law Review* 84:1335–70.

Eichner, M. N. 1988. "Getting Women Work That Isn't Women's Work: Challenging Gender Biases in the Workplace under Title VII." *Yale Law Journal* 97:1397.

Epstein, Lee. 1985. *Conservatives in Court*. Knoxville: University of Tennessee Press.

Estreicher, Samuel. 1996. "Labor and Employment Law." In *Fundamentals of American Law*, edited by A. B. Morrison. Oxford: Oxford University Press.

Fowler, W. Gary. 1984. "Judicial Selection under Reagan and Carter: A Comparison of Their Initial Recommendation Procedures." *Judicature* 67:265.

Frug, M. J. 1992. "Sexual Equality and Sexual Differences in American Law." *New England Law Review* 26:665–82.

Galanter, Marc. 1974. "Why the Haves Come Out Ahead: Speculations on the Limits of Social Change." *Law and Society Review* 9:95–160.

George, Tracey E. 1999. "The Dynamics and Determinants of the Decision to Grant En Banc Review." *Washington Law Review* 74:213–74.

Glick, Henry Robert, and Kenneth N. Vines. 1973. *State Court Systems*. Englewood Cliffs, NJ: Prentice-Hall.

Goldman, Sheldon. 1966. "Voting Behavior on the United States Courts of Appeals, 1961–64." *American Political Science Review* 55:372–83.

———. 1969. "Backgrounds, Attitudes and the Voting Behavior of Judges." *Journal of Politics* 31:214–22.

————. 1975. "Voting Behavior on the United States Courts of Appeal Revisited." *American Political Science Review* 69:491–506.

————. 1989a. "Judicial Appointments and the Presidential Agenda." In *The Presidency in American Politics,* edited by C. B. H. P. Brace and G. King. New York: NYU Press.

————. 1989b. "Reagan's Judicial Legacy: Completing the Puzzle and Summing Up." *Judicature* 72:318–30.

————. 1997. *Picking Federal Judges: Lower Court Selection from Roosevelt through Reagan.* New Haven: Yale University Press.

Goldman, Sheldon, and Elliot Slotnick. 1997. "Clinton's First Term Judiciary: Many Bridges to Cross." *Judicature* 80 (May /June): 254–73.

Gottschall, Jon. 1983. "Carter's Judicial Appointments: The Influence of Affirmative Action and Merit Selection on Voting on the U.S. Court of Appeals." *Judicature* 67:165–73.

————. 1986. "Reagan's Appointments to the U.S. Courts of Appeals: The Continuation of a Judicial Revolution." *Judicature* 48:48–54.

Grossman, Joel B., Herbert M. Kritzer, Kristin Bumiller, Austin Sarat, Stephen McDougal, and Richard Miller. 1982. "Dimensions of Institutional Participation: Who Uses the Courts, and How?" *Journal of Politics* 44:86–114.

Grossman, Joel, and Austin Sarat. 1975. "Litigation in the Federal Courts: A Comparative Study." *Law and Society Review* 9:321–46.

Haire, Susan Brodie. 1993. Judges' Decisions in the United States Courts of Appeals: A Reassessment of Geographic Patterns in Judicial Behavior. Ph.D., University of South Carolina, Columbia.

Haire, Susan B., and Stefanie Lindquist. 1997. "An Agency and Twelve Courts: Social Security Disability Cases in the U.S. Courts of Appeals." *Judicature* March/April: 230–36.

Hall, Melinda Gann, and Paul Brace. 1989. "Order in the Courts: A Neo-Institutional Approach to Judicial Consensus." *Western Political Quarterly* 42:391–407.

————. 1992. "Toward an Integrated Model of Judicial Voting Behavior." *American Politics Quarterly* 20:147–68.

Harrington, Christine B., and Daniel S. Ward. 1995. "Patterns of Appellate Litigation, 1945–1990." In *Contemplating Courts,* edited by L. Epstein. Washington, DC: CQ Press.

Hartley, Roger E., and Lisa M. Holmes. 1997. "Increasing Senate Scrutiny of Lower Federal Court Nominees." *Judicature* 80:274–79.

Haynie, Stacia L. 1992. "Leadership and Consensus on the U.S. Supreme Court." *Journal of Politics* 54:1158–72.

Hill, David B., and Norman R. Luttbeg. 1980. *Trends in American Electoral Behavior.* Itasca, IL: F. E. Peacock.

Hinckley, Barbara. 1983. *Stability and Change in Congress.* New York: Harper and Row.

Horowitz, Donald. 1977. *The Courts and Social Policy.* Washington, DC: Brookings Institute.

Horowitz, Robert B. 1994. "Judicial Review of Regulatory Decisions: The Changing Criteria." *Political Science Quarterly* 109:133–69.

Howard, J. Woodford. 1981. *Courts of Appeals in the Federal Judicial System: A Study of the Second, Fifth and District of Columbia Circuits.* Princeton, NJ: Princeton University Press.

Key, V. O., Jr. 1967. *Public Opinion and American Democracy.* New York: Knopf.

Knibb, David. 1997. *Federal Courts of Appeal Manual: A Manual in Practice in the United States Court of Appeals.* St. Paul, MN: West Publishing.

Kozinski, Alex. 1997. "What I Ate for Breakfast and Other Mysteries of Judicial Decision Making." In *Judges on Judging,* edited by D. M. O'Brien. Chatham: Chatham House.

Lamis, Alexander P. 1988. *The Two Party South.* New York: Oxford University Press.

Landes, William M., and Richard A. Posner. 1980. "Legal Change, Judicial Behavior, and the Diversity Jurisdiction." *Journal of Legal Studies* 9:367.

Low, Peter W., and John C. Jeffries Jr. 1989. *Federal Courts and the Law of Federal-State Relations.* Westbury, NY: Foundation Press.

Marcus, Maeva, and Natalie Wexler. 1992. "The Judiciary Act of 1789: Political Compromise or Constitutional Interpretation?" In *Origins of the Federal Judicairy: Essays on the Judiciary Act of 1789,* edited by M. Marcus. New York: Oxford University Press.

Markus, George B., and Philip E. Converse. 1979. "A Dynamic Simultaneous Equation Model of Electoral Choice." *American Political Science Review* 73:1055–70.

McFeeley, Neil D. 1987. *Appointment of Judges: The Johnson Presidency.* Austin: University of Texas Press.

McIntosh, Wayne. 1983. "Private Use of a Public Forum: A Long Range View of the Dispute Processing Role of Courts." *American Political Science Review* 77:991–1010.

———. 1990. *The Appeal of Civil Law: A Political-Economic Analysis of Litigation.* Urbana: University of Illinois Press.

Mezey, Susan Gluck. 1988. *No Longer Disabled: the Federal Courts and the Politics of Social Security Disability.* New York: Greenwood Press.

Nagel, Stuart S. 1961. "Political Party Affiliation and Judges' Decisions." *American Political Science Review* 55:843–50.

Navasky, Victor S. 1971. *Kennedy Justice.* New York: Atheneum.

Neely, Richard. 1988. *The Product Liability Mess: How Business can be Rescued from the Politics of State Courts.* New York: Free Press.

Niemi, Richard G., and Herbert F. Weisberg. 1984. "Is Party Identification Meaningful?" In *Controversies in Voting Behavior,* edited by Niemi and Weisberg. Washington, DC: Congressional Quarterly Press.

Nye, Mary Alice. 1991. "The U.S. Senate and Civil Rights Roll Call Votes." *Western Political Quarterly* 44:970–86.

Oakley, John B. 1991. "The Screening of Appeals: The Ninth Ciruit's Experience." *Brigham Young University Law Review.*

Pacelle, Richard L., Jr. 1991. *The Transformation of the Supreme Court's Agenda.* San Francisco: Westview Press.

Page, Benjamin I., and Calvin Jones. 1979. "Reciprocal Effects of Policy Preferences, Party Loyalty and the Vote." *American Political Science Review* 73:1071–90.

Parker, Glenn R. 1985. *Studies of Congress.* Washington, DC: Congressional Quarterly Press.

Peltason, J. W. 1961. *Fifty-eight Lonely Men: Southern Federal Judges and School Desegregation.* New York: Harcourt, Brace.

Peters, B. Guy. 1989. *The Politics of Bureaucracy.* 3d ed. New York: Longman.

Pomper, Gerald M. 1975. *Voter's Choice.* New York: Dodd, Mead.

Posner, Richard A. 1985. *The Federal Courts: Crisis and Reform.* Cambridge: Harvard University Press.

———. 1996. *The Federal Courts: Challenge and Reform.* Cambridge: Harvard University Press.

Pound, Roscoe. 1912. "The Scope and Purpose of Sociological Jurisprudence, pt. 3." *Harvard Law Review* 25:489–562.

Pritchett, C. Herman. 1948. *The Roosevelt Court.* New York: Macmillan.

Rehnquist, William H. 1984. "A Plea for Help: Solutions to Serious Problems Currently Experienced by the Federal Judicial System." *St. Louis University Law Journal* 28 (1): 4–5.

Richardson, Richard J., and Kenneth N. Vines. 1970. *The Politics of Federal Courts.* Boston: Little, Brown.

Ripley, Randall B. 1983. *Congress: Process and Policy.* 3d ed. New York: W. W. Norton.

Robinson, Glen O. 1991. *American Bureaucracy: Public Choice and Public Law.* Ann Arbor: University of Michigan Press.

Rohde, David W. 1991. *Parties and Leaders in the Postreform House.* Chicago: University of Chicago Press.

Rosenberg, Gerald N. 1991. *The Hollow Hope: Can Courts Bring About Social Change?* Chicago: University of Chicago Press.

Rowland, C. K., and Robert A. Carp. 1996. *Politics and Judgment in Federal District Courts.* Lawrence: University of Kansas Press.

Rowland, C. K., Donald R. Songer, and Robert A. Carp. 1988. "Presidential Effects on Criminal Justice Policy in the Lower Federal Courts: The Reagan Judges." *Law and Society Review* 22:191–200.

Sarat, Austin, and Joel Grossman. 1975. "Courts and Conflict Resolution: Problems in the Mobilization of Adjudication." *American Political Science Review* 69:1200–1217.

Schuck, Peter H. 1994. *Foundations of Administrative Law.* New York: Oxford University Press.

Schwab, Larry M. 1980. *Changing Patterns of Congressional Politics.* New York: D. Van Nostrand.

Segal, Jeffrey A., and Albert D. Cover. 1989. "Ideological Values and the Votes of U.S. Supreme Court Justices." *American Political Science Review* 83:557–65.

Sharkansky, Ira. 1970. *Regionalism in American Politics.* Indianapolis: Bobbs-Merrill.

Sheehan, Reginald S., William Mishler, and Donald R. Songer. 1992. "Ideology,

Status and the Differential Success of Direct Parties before the Supreme Court." *American Political Science Review* 86:464–71.

Sheehan, Reginald S., and Donald R. Songer. 1989. "Parties before the United States Courts of Appeal in the 1980's." Paper read at Midwest Political Science Association, at Chicago.

Slotnick, Elliot. 1980. "Reforms in Judicial Selection: Will They Affect the Senate's Role?" *Judicature* 64:60–73.

———. 1983. "The ABA Standing Committee on the Federal Judiciary: A Contemporary Assessment—Part 2." *Judicature* 66:385–93.

———. 1988. "Federal Judicial Recruitment and Selection Research: A Review Essay." *Judicature* 71:317–24.

Solomon, R. 1984. "The Politics of Appointment and the Federal Courts' Role in Regulating America: U.S. Courts of Appeals Judgeships from T.R. to F.D.R." *American Bar Foundation Research Journal* 2:285–343.

Songer, Donald R. 1982. "Consensual and Nonconsensual Decisions in Unanimous Opinions of the United States Court of Appeals." *American Journal of Political Science* 26:225–39.

———. 1986. "Factors Affecting Variation in Rates of Dissent in the U.S. Courts of Appeals." In *Judicial Conflict and Consensus: Behavioral Studies of American Courts*, edited by S. Goldman and C. M. Lamb. Lexington: University of Kentucky Press.

———. 1990. "Criteria for Publication of Opinions in the U.S. Court of Appeals: Formal Rules versus Empirical Reality." *Judicature* 73:307–13.

———. 1991. "The Circuit Court of Appeals." In *The American Courts: A Critical Assessment*, edited by J. B. Gates and C. A. Johnson. Washington, DC: C.Q.Press.

Songer, Donald R., and Sue Davis. 1990. "The Impact of Party and Region on Voting Decisions in the United States Courts of Appeals, 1955–1986." *Western Political Quarterly* 43:317–34.

Songer, Donald R., Sue Davis, and Susan Haire. 1994. "A Reappraisal of Diversification in the Federal Courts: Gender Effects in the Courts of Appeals." *Journal of Politics* 56:425–39.

Songer, Donald R., and Susan Haire. 1992. "Integrating Alternative Approaches to the Study of Judicial Voting: Obscenity Cases in the U.S. Court of Appeals." *American Journal of Political Science* 36:963–82.

Songer, Donald R., Jeffrey A. Segal, and Charles M. Cameron. 1994. "The Hierarchy of Justice: Testing a Principal-Agent Model of Supreme Court-Circuit Court Interactions." *American Journal of Political Science* 38:673–96.

Songer, Donald R., and Reginald S. Sheehan. 1990. "Supreme Court Impact on Compliance and Outcomes: Miranda and New York Times in the United States Courts of Appeals." *Western Political Quarterly* 43:297–316.

———. 1992. "Who Wins on Appeal? Upperdogs and Underdogs in the United States Courts of Appeals." *American Journal of Political Science* 36:235–58.

Tate, C. Neal. 1981. "Personal Attribute Model of Voting Behavior of U.S. Supreme Court Justices: Liberalism in Civil Liberties and Economic Decisions, 1946–1978." *American Political Science Review* 75:355–67.

Tate, C. Neal, and Roger Handberg. 1991. "Time Binding and Theory Building in Personal Attribute Models of Supreme Court Voting Behavior, 1916–88." *American Journal of Political Science* 35:460–80.

Tomasi, Timothy B., and Jess A. Velona. 1987. "All the President's Men: A Study of Ronald Reagan's Appointments to the United States Courts of Appeals." *Columbia Law Review* 87:766–93.

Turner, Julius. 1970. *Party and Constituency: Pressures on Congress*, rev. ed. Baltimore: Johns Hopkins University Press.

Ulmer, S. Sidney. 1962. "The Political Party Variable in the Michigan Supreme Court." *Journal of Politics* 11:352–62.

———. 1973. "Social Background as an Indicator to the Votes of Supreme Court Justices in Criminal Cases: 1947–1956 Terms." *American Journal of Political Science* 17:622–30.

———. 1978. "Selecting Cases for Supreme Court Review: An Underdog Model." *American Political Science Review* 78:902–9.

———. 1985. "Government Litigants, Underdogs, and Civil Liberties in the Supreme Court: 1903–1968 Terms." *Journal of Politics* 47:899–909.

Van Winkle, Steven R. 1996. "Three-Judge Panels and Strategic Behavior on the U.S. Courts of Appeals." Paper read at Southern Political Science Association, at Atlanta.

Vines, Kenneth N. 1964. "Federal District Court Judges and Race Cases in the South." *Journal of Politics* 25:337–57.

Walker, Thomas, and Deborah Barrow. 1985. "Diversification of the Federal Bench: Policy and Process Ramifications." *Journal of Politics* 47:596–617.

Weiler, Paul C. 1983. "Promises to Keep: Securing Workers' Rights to Self-Organize under the NLRA." *Harvard Law Review* 96:1769–1827.

Wenner, Lettie McSpadden. 1989. "The Courts and Environmental Policy." In *Environmental Politics and Policy*, edited by J. P. Lester. Durham: Duke University Press.

Wenner, Lettie M., and Lee E. Dutter. 1988. "Contextual Influences on Court Outcomes." *Western Political Quarterly* 41:115–34.

Wheeler, Stanton, Bliss Cartwright Robert Kagan, and Lawrence Friedman. 1987. "Do the Haves Come Out Ahead? Winning and Losing in the State Supreme Courts." *Law and Society Review* 21:403–45.

White, Byron R. 1984. "Dedication—Fifth Circuit Symposium." *Texas Tech Law Review* 15:ix–xi.

Williams, J. C. 1989. "Deconstructing Gender." *Michigan Law Review* 87:797–845.

Woll, Peter. 1985. *Congress*. Boston: Little, Brown.

Wright, Gerald C., Robert S. Erikson, and John P. McIver. 1985. "Measuring State Partisanship and Ideology with Survey Data." *Journal of Politics* 47:469–89.

———. 1987. "Public Opinion and Policy Liberalism in the American States." *American Journal of Political Science* 31:981–99.

———. 1989. "State Political Culture and the Politics of Representation." Paper read at Midwest Political Science Association, at Chicago.

Name Index

Subject and Case Index